Creative Scroll Saw Segmentation

Patrick
Spielman
& Frank A.
Droege

Sterling Publishing Co., Inc.
New York

Library of Congress Cataloging-in-Publication Data

Creative scroll saw segmentation/Patrick Spielman and Frank A. Droege.

p. cm.

ISBN 1-40270-0333-3

1. Jig saws. 2.   Woodwork—Patterns. I. Droege, Frank. II. Title.

TT186 .S66525 2002

684' .08—dc21

2   4   6   8   10   9   7   5   3   1

Published by Sterling Publishing Co., Inc.

387 Park Avenue South, New York, NY 10016

©2003 by Patrick Spielman and Frank Droege

Distributed in Canada by Sterling Publishing

℅ Canadian Manda Group, One Atlantic Avenue, Suite 105

Toronto, Ontario, Canada M6K 3E7

Distributed in Great Britain and Europe by Chrysalis Books

64 Brewery Road, London N7 9NT, England

Distributed in Australia by Capricorn Link (Australia) Pty. Ltd.

P.O. Box 704, Windsor, NSW 2756, Australia

Printed in China

Sterling ISBN 1-40270-0333-3

ACKNOWLEDGMENTS

The authors extend their most sincere thanks and appreciation to our typist Jennifer Blahnik and our graphic artist Roxanne LeMoine. We also wish to acknowledge our spouses Anna Droege and Patricia Spielman for their unwavering support and generous assistance with this work.

Contents

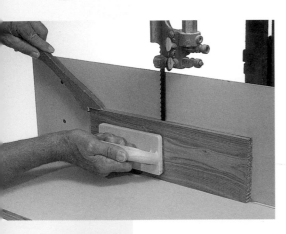

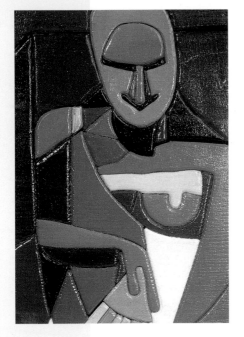

Introduction

The scroll saw is the primary power tool used to make the more than 40 projects in this book. These colorful and imaginative projects were all conceived and created by co-author Frank Droege.

In order to conserve space so that we could include more projects, many of the patterns are presented in a reduced size. They may be enlarged with a photocopier to the size suggested on the pattern or sized to either accommodate material that you may have on hand or to satisfy a special need such as for a lid or cover of a box or a cabinet panel.

Making the projects involves using readily available and inexpensive softwood material, straightforward scroll-sawing techniques, and fundamental woodworking skills. The projects fall into two general categories: those that hang flat against a wall (**I–1** and **I–2**) and those that are freestanding for display on a shelf or table (**I–3**).

The projects, however, are all similar in that they have a "backer." This is usually thin plywood to which various scroll-sawn pieces that have been individually shaped and painted (or stained) have been glued. Scroll-sawers call this category of work "segmentation."

I–1. This Arizona Desert project measures only 3½ × 5¼ inches. Notice how all of its ¼-inch-thick face pieces are flat and level with each other with all of the edges slightly rounded. Each piece was individually painted before being glued to a thin plywood backer.

I–2. Elf with Flowers involves basically the same techniques. However, this project was made from ¾-inch-thick wood and features an integral frame and some segments in relief. This was accomplished by reducing the thickness of the background and other selected "segments."

I–3. This scroll-sawn Kachina Doll is a segmentation project made to look like a one-piece carving. Some segments are reduced, some segments are set forward, and some segments remain at the original level.

WHAT IS SEGMENTATION?

Excluding the plywood or solid-wood backer, the typical segmentation project is made from just one piece of inexpensive softwood (**I–4**). A paper photocopy of a cutting pattern is adhered to the surface and then the workpiece is cut into a number of individual parts or "segments" of an overall design or picture. By and large, there is essentially no waste. The edge of each cutout piece is rounded over or otherwise contoured and then smoothed. Each piece is individually painted or stained before it is glued back into its original space onto a flat backer as part of the total project picture (or standing statuette).

Segmentation should not be confused with a similar but more expensive and labor-intensive process known as "intarsia." Intarsia requires selecting many different kinds and colors of wood that are sometimes exotic species and difficult to obtain. Each piece must be expertly cut, arranged, and fitted to the adjoining pieces. Because of the fine, narrow cuts obtainable with the scroll saw, the inexpensive material, no-waste savings of using just a single board, and the speed and simplicity of single-line cutting are the major advantages of segmentation over intarsia (**I–5**). Many of the project patterns, however, may be converted to intarsia by substituting woods in your choice of suitable natural colors (**I–6**).

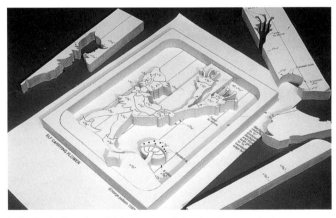

I–5. Reducing the thicknesses of the background pieces sets out the outer frame and brings the Elf and other objects forward in relief.

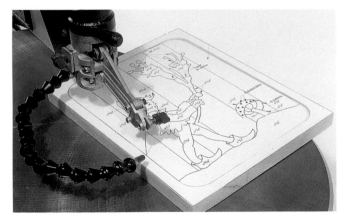

I–4. Most projects begin with a single flat board. Here the pattern has been applied and the workpiece is being sawn into individual segments. All cuts are made directly on the line. There is virtually no waste.

I–6. An example of a basic intarsia project designed and crafted by noted intarsia artist and author Lucille Crabtree. Note that the pieces of wood used were selected for their natural colors.

Chapter 1

Supplies, Tools and Equipment

There are very few essential or special items necessary to get started. Some wood, access to a copy machine, a drill, a scroll saw, and some basic gluing and finishing supplies will get you going. As with any craft, there are always some optional accessories that make one's efforts easier, faster, and just more fun. This chapter provides brief discussions of the essentials and also describes some of the optional accessories.

WOOD MATERIALS

Solid Woods

No. 2 shop pine, northern white cedar, western red cedar, and basswood are very suitable woods and generally easy to obtain (**1–1**). Other domestic softwoods prevalent in your locality should be considered. The basic requirements are that the wood be dry and have some areas without typical defects such as knots and checks. Material stains and defects that can be covered by paint are usually acceptable.

1–1. Pine, red cedar, white cedar, and basswood are good, inexpensive choices for solid wood.

Plywood

Just about any kind of plywood ⅛ to ¼ inch thick is suitable for backer material (**1–2**). Recycled wall paneling is an especially good choice for backing material since it will not be visible and it usually has one good gluing surface. Only tight-core metric plywoods such as Baltic or Finnish birch and poplar should be used for the facing layers that are visible and will be sawn into segments. Solid-core hardwood plywoods are

1–2. On top of ⅛- and ¼-inch-thick sheets of Baltic birch are shown two surfaces of recycled wall paneling—the finished surface on the right and the glueable surface on the left.

generally intended for architectural uses and often chip on the face edges or delaminate when cut into small parts with the scroll saw. Their face veneers are usually poorly glued.

COPY MACHINE

The use of a photocopier is essential for enlarging many of the project patterns. Most public libraries, printing companies, and business communities with a "copy shop" or office-supply store have inexpensive copying services. The better copy machines make enlargements or reductions in one percent increments. Remember that the enlargement sizes given on the pattern pages are merely suggestions. Sometimes a slightly smaller enlargement will allow you to use stock that otherwise may be too small. And, conversely, a slightly larger setting will permit the full use of stock that otherwise would be trimmed with the cutoffs becoming scrap.

PATTERN ADHESIVE

The recommended process is to apply a paper photocopy of the cutting pattern directly to the surface of your wood with a temporary bonding spray adhesive (**1–3**). The saw cuts are then made through the pattern and the wood. A light coat of a good adhesive sprayed only on the back of the pattern should allow it to be removed easily when sawing is completed. If

too much adhesive or a cheap, poor quality or the wrong kind of adhesive is used, it will be necessary to soften the adhesive using a rag and some solvent to soften and remove the pattern.

DRILLING TOOLS

A drill press ensures that the small blade-threading holes needed to cut out inside openings will be made perfectly vertical. A good eye and a square-guided hand drill will also work. Several small fractional or numbered drill bits will get the job done: ¹⁄₁₆- and ¹⁄₃₂-inch diameters are suitable for most sawing jobs. Very fine drill bits with wire gauge numbers 70 to 80 are available to drill holes smaller than ¹⁄₃₂ inch. The larger the number, the smaller the drill.

SCROLL-SAW BLADES

Plain-end blades are definitely recommended over the pin-end types. Skip-tooth, double-tooth, and ground skip-tooth blades are all suitable. The ground blades are not available in sizes smaller than No. 5, which is sometimes too large for many of the projects. Larger-sized blades and the special thick wood blade are best for resawing segments and cutting heavy material (**1–4**). Refer to *The New Scroll Saw Handbook* for a complete discussion of blades, cutting speeds, and useful tips.

1–3. A temporary bond spray adhesive mounts the pattern directly to the workpiece for sawing.

1–4. Basic blades, left to right: No. 2 and No. 5 blades will handle most jobs, and the special thick wood blade is useful but not essential for resawing small pieces to a reduced thickness.

SCROLL SAWS

Almost any scroll saw capable of carrying plain-end blades can be used with success (**1–5** and **1–6**). Saws with a large throat or a thickness-cutting capacity greater than ¾ inch are not required. Saws with a variable-speed control feature and a quick blade-change capability, however, are preferred over single-speed saws. A slower blade-speed option offers better control when sawing thin, soft material. Higher-end

1–5. This 16-inch, reasonably priced saw features variable speed, a light, and up-front controls.

1–6. Another 16-inch, bench-top variable-speed saw features up-front tensioning and a quick blade-change system.

saws are generally more "user friendly," provide less blade breakage, easier blade changes, less vibration, thicker and larger stock-cutting capacities, plus a variety of other conveniences. Refer to *The New Scroll Saw Handbook* for complete descriptions and specifications of scroll saws available today.

Band Saws

A band saw, like a dust-collecting system, is nice to have but not necessary. As discussed in Chapter 2, a band saw is useful for resawing thicker boards into thinner ones that are used to make many of the projects in this book (**1–7**). Thin, solid woods ⅛ and ¼ inch thick, prepared especially for scroll-sawing, are now available from many mail-order houses. This material and imported, metric plywoods are usable and available. They're just more expensive. Refer to Chapter 2, which describes two resawing processes with a band saw.

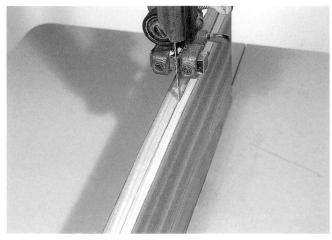

1–7. Having a band saw permits do-it-yourself resawing as shown. However, although more expensive, other thin materials prepared especially for scroll-sawing can be purchased ready to use.

EDGE-FORMING AND SHAPING TOOLS

Once the segments are cut out, the sharp sawn edges need to be rounded over or softened. The amount of round-over or material removal ranges from very little, such as just a 1/16-inch radius on ¼-inch-thick material, to a full ⅜-inch radius on ¾-inch-thick material. Any number of devices can be used, including folded sandpaper or fingernail files (**1–8**) for minimal work, to knives, rasps, and files for greater material removal (**1–9**).

A high-speed rotary tool will greatly speed this work (**1–10**). Various-sized small sanding drums and inexpensive diamond-coated micro-burrs are available that make the rounding over, chamfering, or shaping of all sizes of work very fast and easy (**1–10** to **1–12**.)

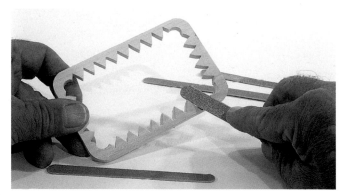

1–8. In a "pinch," fingernail files can be used to slightly soften sawn edges.

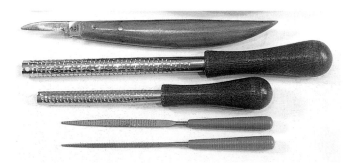

1–9. Various knives, small rasps, and files can be used for greater stock removal, shaping, and detailing.

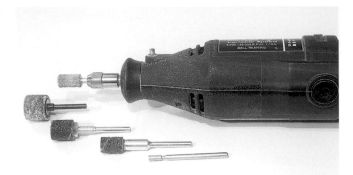

1–10. A high-speed rotary tool has many uses and greatly speeds the work. Accessories with a ⅛-inch shank shown are small drum sanders ¼, ⅜, and ½ inch in diameter; a ⁵⁄₁₆-inch structured carbide cutter mounted in the rotary tool; and a diamond-coated micro-burr shown in the foreground.

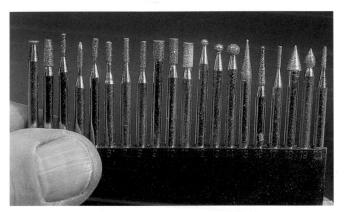

1–11. An inexpensive, yet very serviceable set of 20 different shapes of diamond-coated micro-burrs on ⅛-inch-diameter shanks that cost less than 70 cents each.

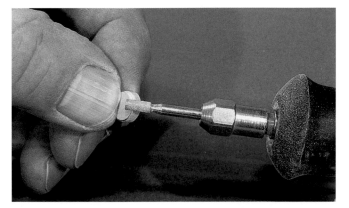

1–12. Using a diamond burr to round over the edges of a very small wood cutout.

ABRASIVES AND SANDING TOOLS

Larger, flat surfaces can be smoothed by employing typical hand-sanding techniques or with power sanders of choice (**1–13** and **1–14**).

1–13. A small pad sander is used to smooth a flat board supported on a nonslip bench pad.

1–14. A random-orbit sander prepares the surface before a cutting pattern is mounted.

PAINTS AND FINISHING SUPPLIES

Water-based paints, such as acrylic art paints, are recommended because of their good shelf life, abundant color choices, good coverage, and easy clean-up (**1–15**). Gel-type stains and slightly thinned acrylic paints allow grain patterns to show through if and when the opportunity presents itself. Some woods, such as basswood, usually have little grain definition. Having some wood filler or water putty on hand is often useful to fill scroll-saw blade-entry holes, dents, chips, and so on. Some cheap sponges and foam and bristle brushes are typical application tools that are also good to have on hand.

1–15. Acrylic paints, brushes, and a paint pencil.

ADHESIVES AND CLAMPING TOOLS

Any one of the many kinds of typical woodworking glues available are satisfactory for these projects. As a general rule, no special adhesives are required, so use whatever kind or type is most familiar.

By and large, special clamping tools are also not an important requirement. Bar clamps are sometimes needed to glue narrow boards edge to edge to make wider panels. Spring clamps, tape, sandbags, or a pile of books or bricks can be used to provide clamping pressure when gluing cut, shaped, and painted segments to the backers. Hand pressure is often sufficient when quick-set or instant adhesives are used.

SAFETY ACCESSORIES

Obviously prudent safety procedures should always be observed in every workshop. Personal protection items, including safety goggles, hearing protectors, and some sort of dust-filtering system are strongly recommended. Other special safety devices to consider include work-holding clamps, push sticks, proper lighting, shop aprons, and, if necessary, proper respirators for protection from any materials that may emit fumes, as well as other hazardous dust or waste. Proper handling, storage, and disposal of flammable materials are other important precautions.

Chapter 2

Techniques: An Overview

GENERAL TECHNIQUES

In almost every craft, there is usually more than one way to accomplish a given task. This is also true when making the segmentation projects in the following chapters. Tooling capabilities and materials available vary from workshop to workshop and each craftperson must work within their own limitations. Individual experimentation is encouraged to personalize and streamline the procedures described in this chapter.

Working in a fully equipped shop affords the luxury of performing more and different procedures than working in one with just the bare essentials of a scroll saw and hand drill. This is especially true when preparing the material for a project. If a table saw, jointer, planer, and band saw are not available to prepare the wood, then purchasing stock of the correct size and thickness becomes the primary option. Substituting suitable plywood may be another workable possibility (**2–1**).

2–1. Preparing material for making small projects such as this may involve different procedures than employed to make larger panels.

Preparing Material

The projects in this book are made from solid wood and/or plywood materials ranging from ⅛ to ¾ inch in thickness. If plywood is used, it only needs to be selected for thickness and quality and then sawn to appropriate width and length. When preparing solid-wood boards, they need to be machined to thickness and sometimes a number of pieces must be glued edge-to-edge to make a necessary width.

■ Resawing

Resawing (**2–2** and **2–3**) is the process of sawing solid wood to thickness. Resawing techniques may be necessary to make up project panels that will be subsequently scroll-sawn into the project's segments. Resawing techniques may also be applied to reduce the thicknesses of selected segmented pieces to create relief on the project's face surfaces.

This class of resawing work is discussed later. There are various ways to resaw boards on the band saw. Two not so common, but effective, techniques follow: *Technique No. 1* simply involves following a straight line marked on the edge of a board. To keep the board vertical and prevent it from tipping during cutting, a clamp or drill-press vise provides steady support (**2–4** and **2–5**).

2–2. When a board is resawn to thickness, it is supported on its edge. Here is a closeup of a band saw making a resawing cut along a marked edge.

2–3. Resawing almost always results in two or more usable pieces from one board.

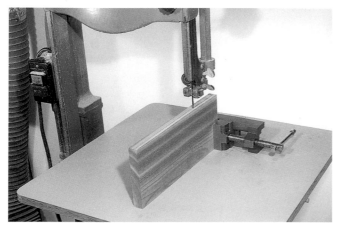

2–4. Resawing technique No. 1: A line is followed freehand with the work supported at the starting end with the aid of a small vise.

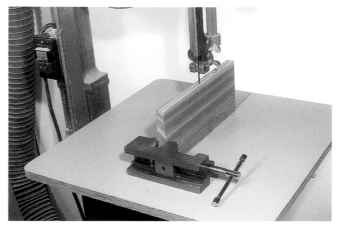

2–5. The vise is moved to the uncut end to complete the cut. The resulting cuts are surprisingly accurate.

Technique No. 2 is a more involved process using a shop-made fence (**2–6** and **2–7**). The advantage of this technique is that once the fence is set up, duplicate thicknesses can be sawn quickly and without marking a cutting line or the shifting clamps and/or vises. General construction details for making a typical fence and an auxiliary table for a 14-inch band saw are given in **2–8**.

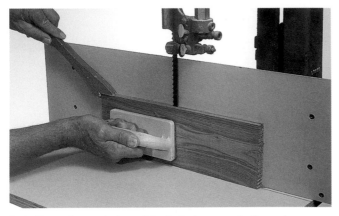

2–6. Resawing technique No. 2: A shop-made fence is clamped to the saw table so it compensates for blade "lead." The fence supports and guides the workpiece as shown.

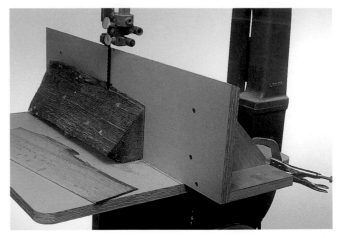

2–7. Sometimes chunks of dry, dead wood may be economically sawn into boards as shown.

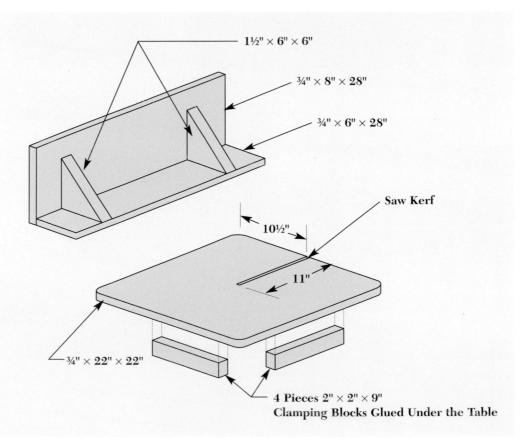

2–8. Details for making an auxiliary band-saw table and a high fence.

1½" × 6" × 6"

¾" × 8" × 28"

¾" × 6" × 28"

Saw Kerf

10½"

11"

¾" × 22" × 22"

4 Pieces 2" × 2" × 9"
Clamping Blocks Glued Under the Table

Most band saws tend to cut with some "lead" toward one side, so a slight angular feed direction is necessary to compensate. To determine the amount of lead and how to set the fence to correct for lead, proceed as follows:

1. Select a scrap board with a straight edge and draw a cutting line about one to two inches parallel to that edge.
2. With a freehand feed, saw along this line. You will soon be compensating your feed direction to correct for "lead." With the blade still in the cut, stop the feed and shut down the saw while holding the board down against the table at the feeding angle. Now, draw a pencil line onto the table following the straight edge of the board.
3. Set and clamp your fence at the resawing thickness (distance from the blade) and with the fence also in a position that is parallel to the line drawn on the table.
4. Make successive resawing cuts as necessary. Keep the stock against the fence with some side pressure (**2–6** and **2–7**).

Smoothing Band-Sawn Surfaces

Surfaces cut with the band saw can be smoothed with a planer, a drum-sanding machine, a portable electric sander (**2–9**) or, if need be, by hand. Workpiece surfaces should be sanded smooth before applying cutting patterns.

Edge-to-Edge Gluing

Depending upon the panel size required and the resawing capacity of the band saw, edge gluing may be done (if necessary) either before or after resawing (**2–10**). In either case, the gluing edges should be machined straight and true with a jointer or a hand plane.

2–9. Sanding to smooth and flatten a resawn surface.

2–10. Boards glued edge-to-edge to make a wide panel.

PROJECT TECHNIQUES

Adhering Patterns

Enlarge the pattern as desired assuring that it will cover the stock (panel size) on hand. Trim the pattern to size with scissors. Apply a light coat of temporary bonding spray adhesive to the back of the pattern and press it to the best surface of your stock (**2–11**).

Drilling Blade-Threading Holes

Drilling blade-threading holes is a necessary step when making inside cutouts. Holes can be drilled either directly on the line or just to either side of it (**2–12**). Drilling to one side of the line offers the advantage that if you want to later fill the hole, or the remaining part of it, you need to work on only one piece or segment (refer to **2–16**). Generally, however, when holes are drilled directly on the line, the kerf will consume most of the hole and any small indents remaining will likely be filled with paint or be visually insignificant.

Auxiliary Zero-Clearance Table

Sawing very small pieces is a frequent task, and it is easily accomplished when the work is supported all around the blade. Drill a small hole for the blade in some thin sheet material such as plastic, hardboard, or plywood. Then secure it to the scroll-saw table with masking tape (**2–13**) or with double-faced tape (**2–14**). This setup prevents small cut pieces from falling through the table opening (**2–15**).

Sawing the segments is best done whenever possible with a No. 2 blade, even when sawing material ¼ to ¾ inch in thickness. A No. 2 blade cuts a very narrow kerf and any gaps between sawn segments will be almost totally eliminated when the segments and their edges are coated with paint and glued in place (**2–16** to **2–18**).

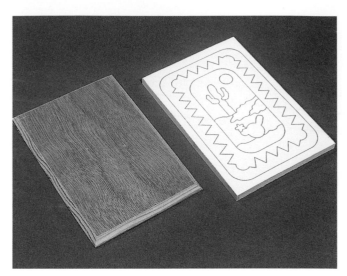

2–11. A project prepared and ready for sawing. Left: The plywood backer with a bevel-sawn edge. Right: A scissor-trimmed pattern is aligned to the edges and bonded to the workpiece.

2–12. Drilling a ⅟₃₂-inch blade-entry hole located to one side of the cutting line.

2–13. A piece of ⅛-inch-thick hardboard is used for this zero-clearance auxiliary table, which is held in place with tape.

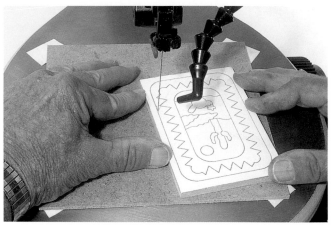

2–14. Scroll-sawing the integral frame of a typical project. Notice that the zero-clearance table held in place with double-faced tape does not interfere with regular scroll-saw work.

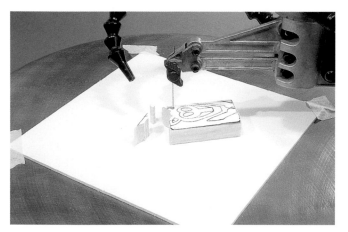

2–15. Extremely small cutout parts remain supported on the auxiliary saw table and will not become lost.

2–16. This small hollow remaining from a blade-entry hole will be hidden when filled and painted.

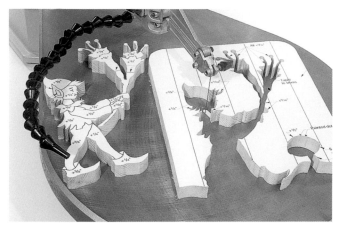

2–17. Fine details can be cut in even ¾-inch-thick softwood stock using a No. 2 skip-tooth blade.

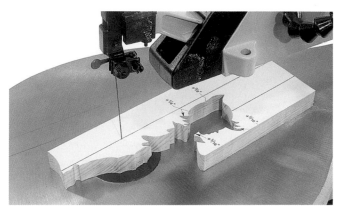

2–18. Even long, straight lines such as these background division lines can be accurately cut freehand in thick softwood stock using narrow blades.

Reducing Thicknesses of Segments

Reducing thicknesses of segments is sometimes required so adjoining areas of selected segments may project outward from others to be in relief. Relief on segmentation project surfaces can be achieved by either placing prepared shims under certain segments or reducing the thicknesses of others. Thicknesses can be reduced with belt- or disc-sanding machines or by sawing with a band saw or scroll saw. Since most segments are of relatively small size and much too dangerous to machine, especially with the band saw, scroll-saw resawing is the best method.

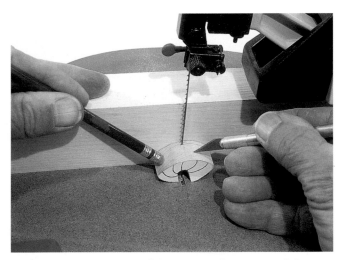

2–19. Resawing a group of six very small segments (left together in one piece) all to the same thickness. Here a combined resawing fence and auxiliary table accessory is used. Note the wide "thick wood" cutting blade.

Scroll-saw resawing small segments (**2–19**) can be done freehand or with the aid of a shop-made fence accessory. Resawing with or without the fence, it is always helpful to mark the edges all around each segment indicating how much material needs to be removed. This is easily accomplished with a shop-made "scribbing" jig (**2–20**). Illus. **2–21** provides a full-size cutting and drilling pattern that can be permanently glued to a block of hardwood.

The shop-made ripping/resawing fixture has a fence permanently secured to an auxiliary table (**2–22** to **2–24**). Because most scroll-saw blades, like band-saw blades, tend to track slightly to one side, the feed direction may need to be slightly angular to compensate for the lead. Review the setup procedures as explained for setting up a resawing fence for the band saw as described under "Technique No. 2" on pages 16 and 17 (**2–25** and **2–26**).

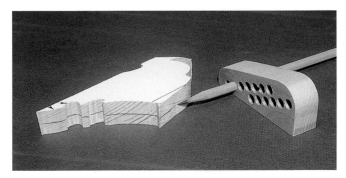

2–20. A shop-made "scribbing" jig in use.

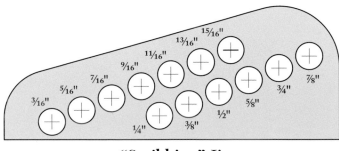

"Scribbing" Jig

Full-Size Pattern

2–21. "Scribbing" jig full-size pattern.

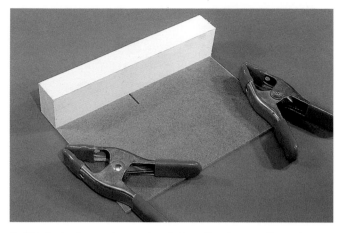

2–22. A ripping and resawing fixture for the scroll saw is easy to make.

2–23. The ripping and resawing fixture shown clamped to the scroll-saw table.

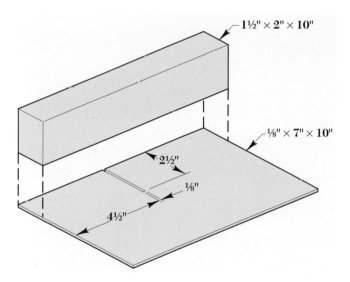

1½" × 2" × 10"

⅛" × 7" × 10"

2½"

⅛"

4½"

2–24. Details for making the ripping/resawing fixture.

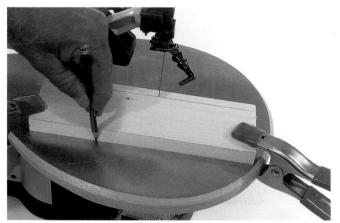

2–25. Checking a scroll-saw blade for "lead." Notice the blade in the cutting line (drawn in red) parallel to the right edge of this board while held in place with the power off. A line parallel to the cut is drawn onto the surface of the saw table.

2–26. With the fence surface adjusted parallel to the line marked onto the saw table, clamp the fixture in place. Here a fairly large background segment is being resawn to a reduced thickness with the scroll saw.

After all of the segments have been cut out and those to be reduced or resawn have been attended to, it's time to round over the edges. Remember to leave the patterns attached as long as possible. If you have removed stock from the faces of some segments, it may be helpful to mark the back surfaces with an "X" to keep all of the front surfaces properly oriented.

The majority of projects require removing just a minimum of material from the face edges of each segment in the rounding-over process. The actual radius or chamfer is usually only about ⅟₃₂ to ⅟₁₆ inch, which makes about an ⅛-inch-wide indent all along the lines between two adjoining segments. Larger projects could be slightly more. Use a high-speed rotary tool for the fastest and best results.

Small sanding drums (**2–27**) and diamond burrs (**2–28**) must be moved over the edges quickly with a fairly rapid, back-and-forth action and very little pressure. Use a very light and quick rubbing action. A hesitation or slow feed with the tool engaged on the work will result in a deep cut and an uneven edge. Illus. **2–28** illustrates a pretty straightforward technique for rounding over the edges of very small segments. *Tip:* If diamond burrs or sanding drums load up with pitch or resin, they can be cleaned by running the tool against an "abrasive cleaning stick" of the type used to clean and renew belt and disc sanders, or the residue can be burned off with a torch.

Coarse-grit sanding drums and structured carbide cutters should be used only to remove greater amounts of material. This type of power cutting is

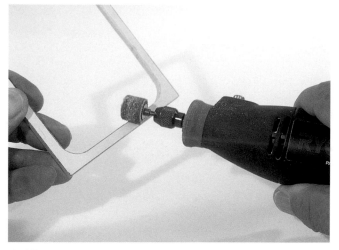

2–27. Using a small drum sander in a high-speed rotary tool to round the inside edge of the frame piece (segment) for a small project. Notice that the pattern is still on the wood.

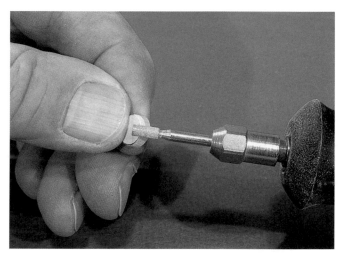

2–28. Even the smallest of segmented pieces are safely and quickly rounded over using diamond-coated micro-burrs in a high-speed rotary tool.

ideal for shaping various surfaces and segments of standing statuettes (**2–29**) and for projects such as those shown in **2–36** and **2–37**.

Final smoothing and sanding work should require minimum effort, if any. The diamond mini-burrs can be used to smooth surfaces initially rounded over with coarser-grit sanding drums and/or coarser structured carbide cutters. Remove any patterns or pattern pieces still attached to the wood (**2–30**). If too much adhesive or the wrong kind was used, soften the adhesive with lacquer thinner or mineral spirits.

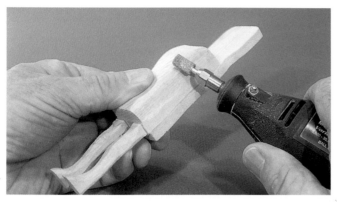

2–29. Carving knives, rasps, or fast-cutting structured carbide tooling can be used for more major rounding over or material removing and shaping jobs such as this.

2–30. Properly applied patterns should remove easily; otherwise, use appropriate solvents to soften the adhesive.

Painting and Assembly

Refer to the project photos for recommended paint color and finish selections. Water-based paints are recommended because of their ease of use. It's best to apply a base coat of regular acrylic white house paint primer (**2–31** and **2–32**). Follow this with a light sanding to remove all raised fibers. For stained projects, it is suggested that water-based stains be considered.

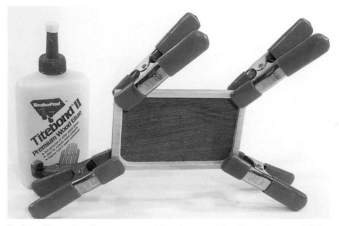

2–31. Glue the frame to a thin plywood backer piece, which should be cut slightly smaller (⅛ inch all around) with its edges beveled back 30 to 45 degrees.

2–32. Painting the frame (border) after it is glued to the backer. Be sure to coat all visible edges and only the rear surface of the backer.

Multiple color finishes such as that shown in **2–33** will be seen on some projects. These finishes are easier to create than they look. Simply apply a base coat of a selected color. Then use small pieces of sponge (premoistened with water for acrylic paints) and dab on the second or third colors, making a random pattern (**2–34**).

2–33. A sponge finish has been applied to the multiple colored segments on this project.

2–34. Applying the second color in a sponge finish with a sponge and a "dabbing" action.

Special Techniques

Individual creative expression in shaping and painting is encouraged. Additional detailing, for example, can be achieved by just painting a white dot on an eye, using a wood-burning tool to groove and texture surfaces, or add definition lines on unpainted wood surfaces, and so on. Illus. **2–35** to **2–38** provide a few ideas.

Complete each project with the application of a clear, satin acrylic spray top coat. Add a saw-tooth wall hanger to the back of the project or install other hardware as necessary.

2–35. An example of a finished project featuring an integral frame and a reduced background level that elevates the sculptured flower in relief.

2–36. A closeup look at the flower detail shows that some of its segments are at different thickness levels and that they are also creatively rounded over or shaped.

2–37. This closeup shows some creative techniques: A band saw was used to make the wide kerf definition cuts in the bow and hair, and major rounding-over techniques shape the balloons and other segments. Wire was used for the balloon "strings."

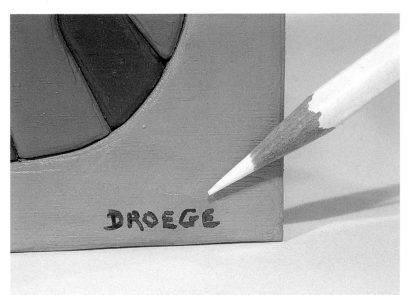

2–38. It's important to sign your work so that the artist can be identified today and in future generations.

Chapter 3

Flat Work

Cats and Cardinals. See pages 38 and 39 for project.

This chapter provides nine easy-to-make projects. All of the projects have similar construction details in that they have integral sawn frames and the face surfaces are flat. That is, no piece or pieces are set out from others in relief. Relief features, however, can be added, if desired, by simply inserting thin shims under selected segments.

The plywood backers are sawn slightly less in size than the project's width and length. The backer's edges are bevel-sawn at 30 to 45 degrees. Unless specified otherwise, the facing material is ¼-inch-thick solid wood or Baltic birch plywood.

Once you have the pattern sized and the material prepared, follow these simple steps:

1. Cut out all of the segments as per the pattern using a No. 2 reverse-tooth or 2/0 scroll-saw blade.
2. Round over the sawn edges to a ⅓₂- to ⅟₁₆-inch radius.
3. Paint the face surfaces and edges of the segments.
4. Glue the frame to the backer and then glue the painted segments to the backer.

Refer to Chapter 2 for more detailed and illustrated instructional techniques. Use the photo provided with each project to assist with color and finishing selections.

3–1. Arizona Desert.

Arizona Desert

Full-Size Pattern

3–2. Use ¼-inch material with a ⅛-inch backer.

3–3. Brown-Eyed Susan.

3–4. Use ¼-inch material with a ⅛-inch backer.

Brown-Eyed Susan   **Full-Size Pattern**

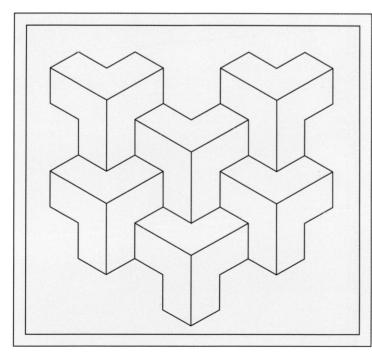

Tumbling Blocks   **Full-Size Pattern**

3–5. Tumbling Blocks.

3–6. Use ¼-inch material with a ⅛-inch backer.

3–7. I'm Ready.

I'm Ready

Enlarge pattern 125%

3—8. Use ¼-inch material with a ⅛- or ¼-inch backer.

3–9. Night & Day nautical scene.

Night & Day Nautical Scene

Enlarge Pattern 150%

3–10. Use ¼-inch material with a ¼-inch backer.

3–11. Star & Anchor nautical symbols.

Star & Anchor Nautical Symbols

Enlarge Pattern 130%
Note: All Stock ¼" Thick

3–12. Use ¼-inch material with a ¼-inch backer.

3–13. Boy Fishing. Notice the painted brown dots on the yellow flowers and the white stripes painted on the bobber.

3–14. This closeup shows real fine thread glued at the pole and bobber after painting and assembly.

Boy Fishing

Enlarge Pattern 145%

3–15. Use ¼-inch material with a ¼-inch backer.

3–16. Cats and Cardinals. Notice that the edges of all of the cats and cardinals *are not* rounded over. Holes are drilled into the birdhouses.

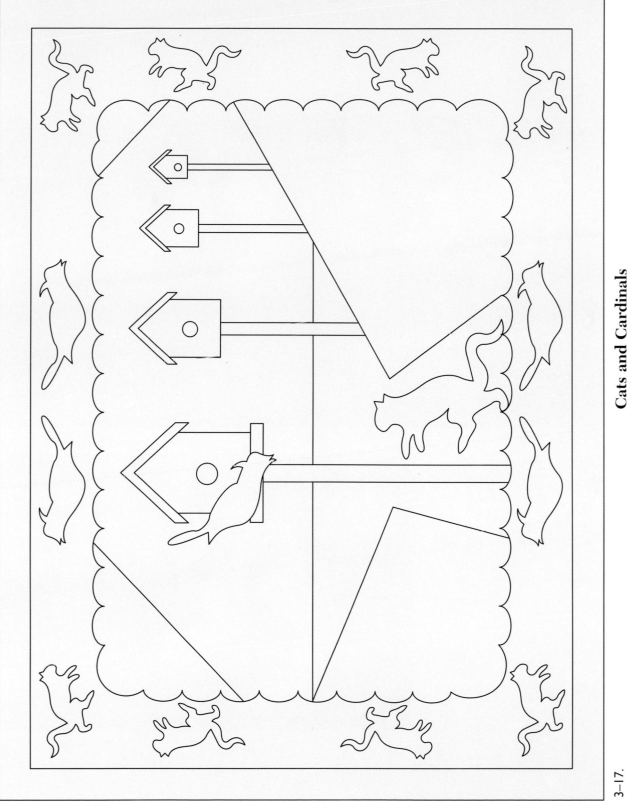

Cats and Cardinals
Enlarge Pattern 125%

3–17.

3–18. Puffins.

3–19. Closeup of Puffins. The eyes are painted dots.

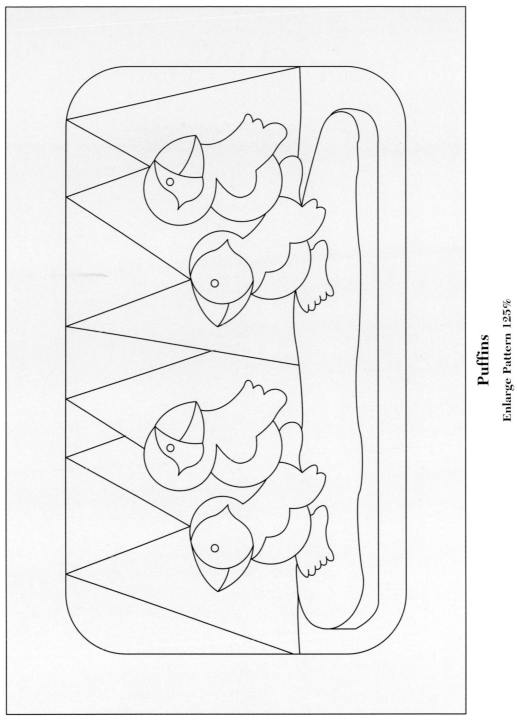

3–20. Use ¼-inch material with ¼-inch backer.

Fine Art Reproductions

4–1. "Cornfield and Crows" by Vincent Van Gogh.

Paintings by the world's master painters are the subjects for the eight projects in this chapter. Now, you can use your scroll saw to recreate the works of Vincent Van Gogh, Pablo Picasso, and other all-time, great painters. The artists would undoubtedly be thrilled to see their work translated into wood, and we assume everyone will like these segmented versions as well.

The projects are all straightforward, flat works. To make these unusual projects, employ the same techniques discussed on page 27 of Chapter 3 and review the general techniques discussed in Chapter 2.

4–2. Use ¼-
inch material
with ¼-inch
backer.

Enlarge Pattern 120%

"Cornfield and Crows"

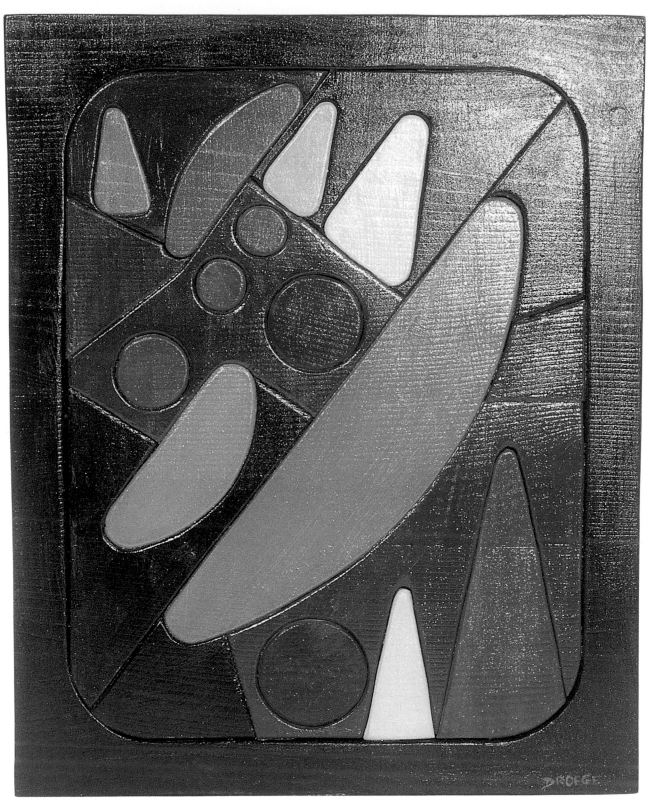

4–3. ''Rain'' by Auguste Herbin.

"Rain" **Enlarge Pattern 125%**

4–4. Use ¼-inch material with ¼-inch backer.

4–5. "Woman with a Fan" by Pablo Picasso.

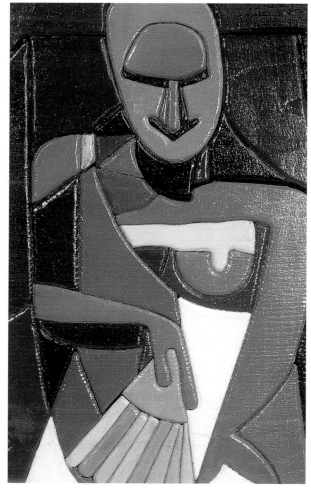

4–6. A closeup of "Woman with a Fan."

"Woman with a Fan"

Enlarge Pattern 140%

4–7. Use ¼-inch material with ¼-inch backer.

4–8.
"Man Seated"
by Roger de la
Fresnaye.

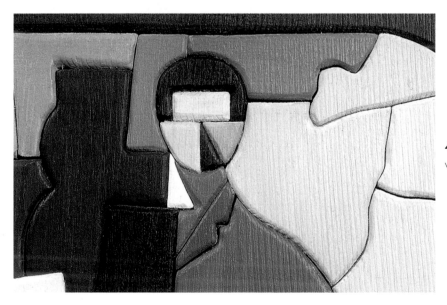

4–9. A closeup of "Man Seated." Notice the visible wood grain.

"Man Seated" Enlarge Pattern 125%

4–10. Use ¼-inch material with ¼-inch backer.

4–11. "Dancers" by Henri Matisse.

4–12. A closeup of "Dancers." Wide kerfs are left as open spaces against black painted areas of the backer.

4–13. Use ¼-inch material with ¼-inch backer.

4–14. "Cornfield with Cypresses" by Vincent Van Gogh.

4–15. A closeup of "Cornfield with Cypresses." Be sure to sign your projects.

"Cornfield with Cypresses"

Full-Size Pattern (or Enlarge Up to 160%)

4–16. Use ¼-inch material with ¼-inch backer.

4–17. "The Scream" by Edvard Munch.

4–18. A closeup of "The Scream." Painted dots highlight the eyes and indicate the nose.

4–19. Blade-entry holes are slightly detectable on the eye and mouth cuts, but do not greatly detract from this work.

4–20. Use ¼-inch material with ¼-inch backer.

"The Scream"   **Enlarge Pattern 130%**

4–21. "Self Portrait" by Vincent Van Gogh.

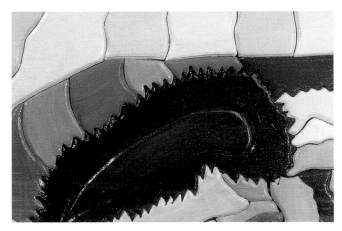

4–22. A closeup of "Self Portrait."

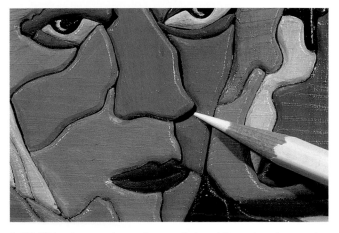

4–23. This closeup shows how a little white paint gives realistic detail to the eyes.

"Self Portrait"

Enlarge Pattern 140%

4-24. Use ¼-inch material with ¼-inch backer.

Chapter 5

Plaques with Relief and Frames

Projects with some of the cutout segments set forward at various levels of relief have greater visual impact than those that are all flat or made with every piece at the same level. The dimensional or relief effect is generally fairly easy to achieve. A particular segment can be raised in two ways: by cutting out a small shim of thin plywood and gluing it under the segment; or by lowering the adjoining segments or surrounding background pieces by reducing their thicknesses. In both instances, the projects are still made with some type of backer to which segments and background pieces are glued.

The project descriptions that follow will provide brief material requirements and discuss special procedures where necessary. The patterns also provide some instructions. A plus (+) symbol with a fraction indicates the amount the segment should be elevated. A minus (-) symbol indicates how much material should be removed. Segments without any instructions are left at the same thickness as the material used when starting.

5–1. This Bicycle Racer project is made with ¾-inch-thick material, including ¾-inch-thick backer (for the plaque).

Bicycle Racer

This project (**5–1** and **5–2**) begins with two pieces of ¾-inch-thick solid wood: one 9¼ × 11½-inch backer piece and one 7¼ × 8½-inch piece that will be sawn into segments. This project features a large plaque backer that is visible. Some segments are reduced, and some remain the full ¾-inch thickness. Edges are rounded over to about a ⅛-inch radius. Routing a decorative edge around the backer plaque is optional.

5–2. Pattern for Bicycle Racer.

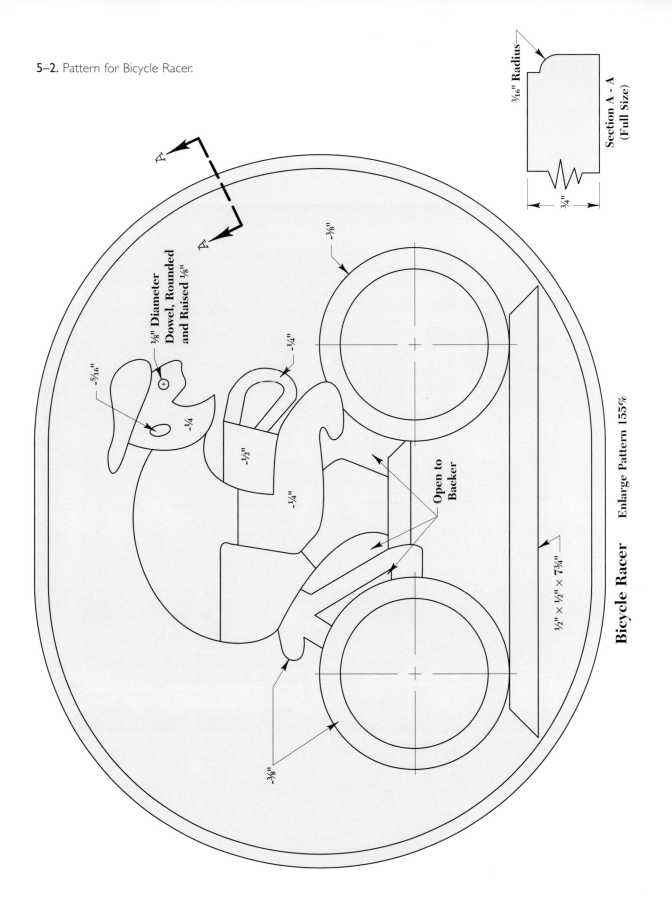

3/16" Radius

Section A - A
(Full Size)

3/4

1/8" Diameter
Dowel, Rounded
and Raised 1/8"

−5/16"

−1/4

−1/2"

−1/4"

−1/4"

−3/8"

Open to
Backer

−3/8"

1/2" × 1/2" × 7 3/4"

Bicycle Racer   Enlarge Pattern 155%

Sailboat and Whale

This project (**5–3** and **5–4**) requires a piece of ⅜-inch-thick 8 × 10-inch material and a ¼-inch-thick backer. A 31-inch length of ⅜-inch-diameter nylon rope is glued into a channel cut out with the scroll saw. The overlaid whale conceals the rope-end butt joint. Saw shims from ¼-inch plywood to elevate the segments as identified on the pattern.

5–3. Sailboat and Whale project that features an inlay of real rope and some segments in relief.

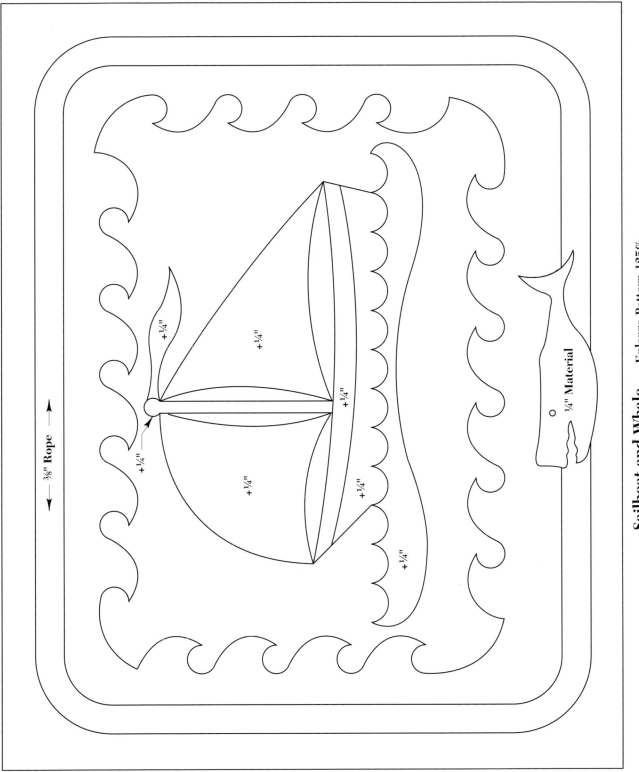

Sailboat and Whale   Enlarge Pattern 125%

¼ Material

⅜" Rope

+¼"

5–4. Use ⅜-inch-thick material with ¼-inch backer.

Lovable Puppy

This is a small project (**5–5** to **5–7**) measuring just 3½ × 4¼ inches, but the pattern can be enlarged to any size desired. To make the project as shown, use ½-inch-thick solid-wood stock and a ⅛-inch-thick solid-wood backer. The steps are:

1. Stack-cut the outside profiles of both the backer and face so their outside profile shapes are the same.
2. Set the backer aside and saw the face into segments as per the pattern.
3. Reduce the thicknesses of those segments as specified on the pattern.
4. Round over and shape each segment, smooth and glue nonpainted segments to the backer, and stain all stained segments and the edges of the backer.
5. Glue in painted segments and paint the nose to include the backer edge (**5–6**).

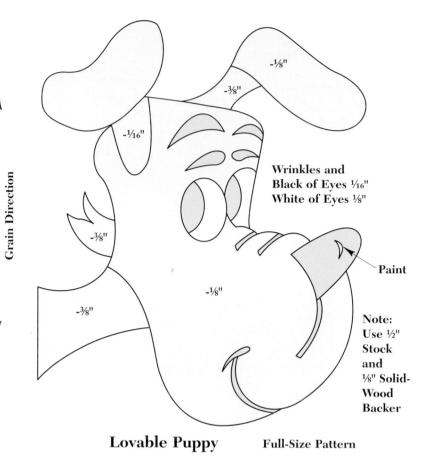

Grain Direction

-⅛"
-⅜"
-1/16"
-⅜"
-⅛"
-⅜"

Wrinkles and Black of Eyes 1/16"
White of Eyes ⅛"

Paint

Note: Use ½" Stock and ⅛" Solid-Wood Backer

Lovable Puppy   **Full-Size Pattern**

5–7. Use ½-inch solid-wood stock and ⅛-inch solid-wood backer. Notice that the puppy's right ear and nose are the only pieces remaining at a full ½-inch thickness.

5–5. Lovable Puppy.

5–6. Painted segments are glued in after the project and visible edge of the backer are stained. The nose is painted to include the edge of the backer and then highlighted with a streak of white paint.

62

Lighthouse in a Shell

This little nautical treasure (**5–8** and **5–9**) was made from a piece of ½ × 3½ × 4½-inch solid wood. There is no separate backer piece. First, saw the border free; then reduce the thicknesses of the inside segments as specified on the pattern. No serious effort was made to round over any of the edges. Sand, stain, and assemble the pieces with droplets of glue.

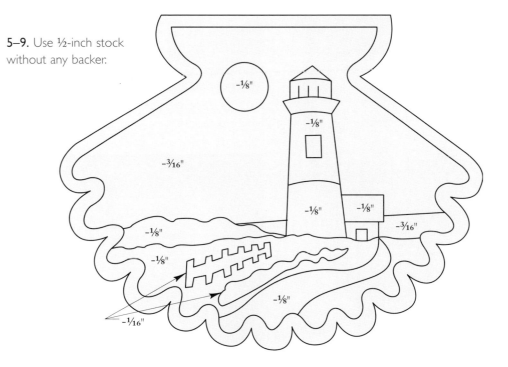

5–8. Lighthouse in a Shell is another small project that can be made larger if desired.

5–9. Use ½-inch stock without any backer.

Lighthouse in a Shell

Pattern Full-Size for ½" Thick Material
Option: Enlarge as Desired

Northern Indian Mask

This colorful project (**5–10** to **5–18**) involves shimming some segments, reducing the thicknesses of others, and leaving some at their original thickness. A piece of ¾ × 6 × 7½-inch softwood and a ¼-inch-thick plywood backer are used. A little creative carving or shaping to round over the outside edges and to form the nose, lips, and eyes is required, but this is not difficult work. Study **5–10** to **5–18**.

Notice that the contour all around the outside edges is rounded over to about a ⅜-inch radius. Then the edges of the segments extending into these areas are rounded over to about a ¹⁄₁₆-inch radius. The two diamond-shaped segments located to the lower side of the nose have thinly painted detailing lines on their surfaces. Also notice the "splash" of red painted around the eyes.

5–10. Northern Indian Mask.

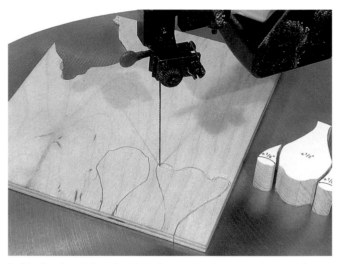

5–11. Sawing shims for the three raised nose segments from ¼-inch plywood.

5–12. With shims under the segments, mark the level of the adjoining surfaces

5–13. Use ¾-inch solid-wood stock and ¼-inch-thick plywood backer. Note: taper the nose pieces. The dashed lines indicate the start of slanted surfaces toward the eyes.

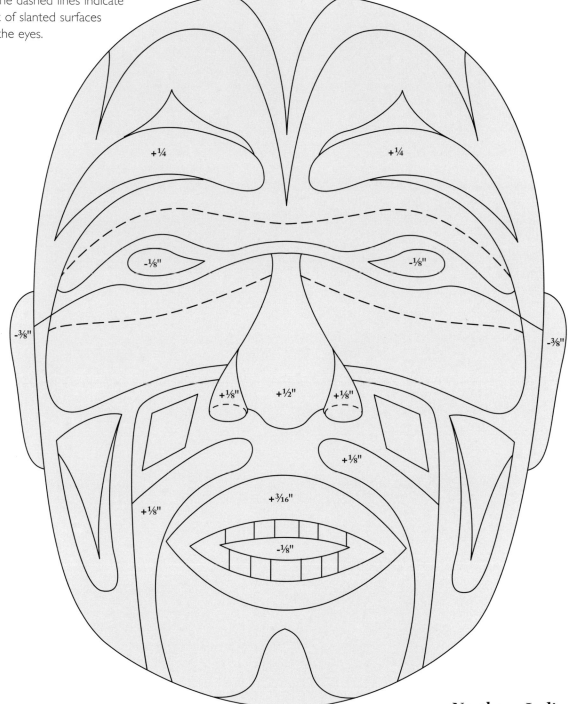

+¼

+¼

-⅛"

-⅛"

-⅜"

-⅜"

+⅛"

+½"

+⅛"

+⅛"

+⅛"

+³⁄₁₆"

-⅛"

Notes:
1. Taper Nose Pieces
2. Slant from Dashed Lines Toward Eyes

Northern Indian Mask

Full-Size Pattern

5–14. Closeup look at the tapered nose and the surfaces slanting toward the nose.

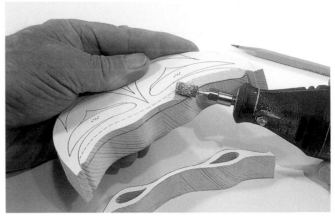

5–15. Tapering the slanted surfaces using a rotary tool and cutter.

5–16. Tapering of the nose pieces and the tapering around the eyes are completed before the pieces are sawed, the patterns are removed, and the other segments are sawn out.

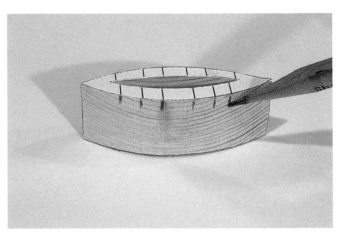

5–17. Locating tooth lines on the sawn edges.

5–18. Use a wood burner or the corner of a file to form tooth-line indentations.

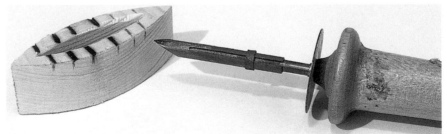

Springtime Flowers

This project (**5–19** and **5–20**) requires a piece of ¾ × 7⅜ × 8½-inch solid wood and a ¼-inch plywood backer the same size. First, saw the frame piece free and glue it to the backer. The flowers, leaves, and stems are all set forward in relief to the background. This is accomplished by resawing the background pieces to a reduced thickness of ½ inch after the other segments have been cut out and set aside.

The flowers and larger leaf segments *are not* reduced in thickness. The light-green stems are reduced about ⅛ inch, as are the two lower leaves painted dark-green. Round over the edges of the background pieces, and paint and glue them to the backer inside the frame. All pieces are rounded over appropriately with a 1/16- to ⅛-inch radius and sanded, painted, and glued inside the reduced background pieces.

5–19. Springtime Flowers. Reducing the background pieces sets the flowers, stems, and leaves out in relief.

Springtime Flowers

Enlarge Pattern 115%

5–20. Pattern for Springtime Flowers. Use ¾ × 7⅜ × 8½-inch solid wood and a ¼-inch plywood backer.

Tulip and Bulb

This project (**5–21** to **5–23**) requires one piece of ¾ × 3½ × 9⅜-inch solid wood and a ⅛- or ¼-inch plywood backer the same size. This project, like the "Springtime Flowers" project, brings segments and the frame into relief by reducing the thickness of the inside background. The two red segments of the flower and the brown bulb piece have ¼-inch-thick shims under them so they stand out ¼ inch further than the frame and ½ inch from the background segments. The dark-green leaf segments are reduced approximately ⅛ inch. Round over and shape the pieces as appropriate (**5–22**).

5–22. This closeup shows the shaping of the tulip. Pieces in red are raised with shims.

5–21. Tulip and Bulb is made exactly the same as the Springtime Flowers, except that ¼-inch-thick shims were glued under the tulip and bulb segments to increase the relief.

5–23. Pattern for Tulip and Bulb. Use ¾ x 3½ x 9⅜-inch solid wood and a ⅛- or ¼-inch plywood backer.

Tulip and Bulb

Enlarge Pattern 111%

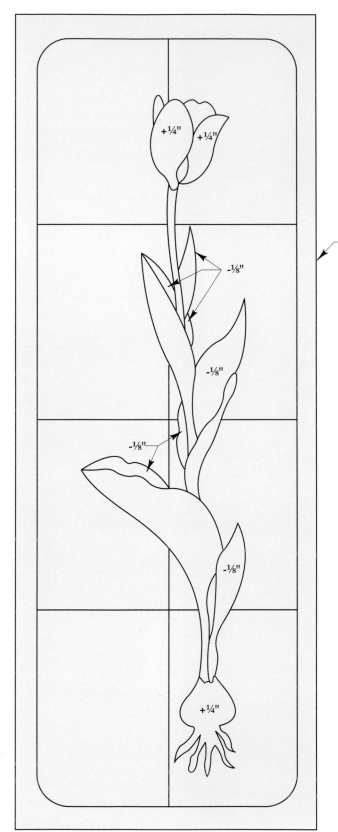

+¼" +¼"

¾" Stock. Background Reduced to ½" Thickness. Both Glued to ⅛" or ¼" Beveled Edge Backer

-⅛"

-⅛"

-⅛"

-⅛"

+¼"

Horn of Plenty

This project (**5–24** to **5–26**) was made from one piece of ¾ × 7⅜ × 9¼-inch solid wood, and a piece of ¼-inch plywood the same size. This project features a double frame with slightly raised apples. Drill the small blade-entry holes where the stem meets the apple. Use a No. 2 reverse-tooth or a 2/0 blade. The stems are actually small indentations carved or filed into the frame and then painted green.

Other features of this project include the resawn background pieces that elevate the cutout segments, the use of a wood-burning tool to indent the veins of the leaves, and the definition lines on the pumpkins and the horn.

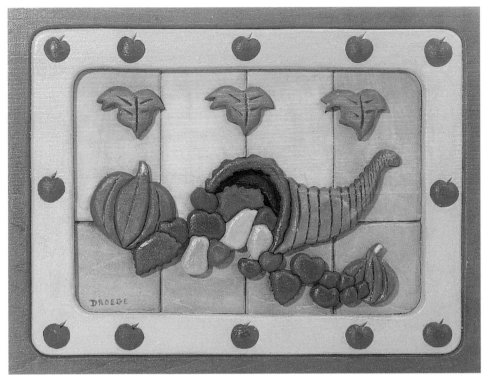

5–24. Horn of Plenty. Notice the interesting double frame featuring slightly raised apples.

5–25. This closeup shows that the stems of the apples are actually small V-shaped indents carved into the frame and painted green. The lines on the pumpkin and horn were wood-burned.

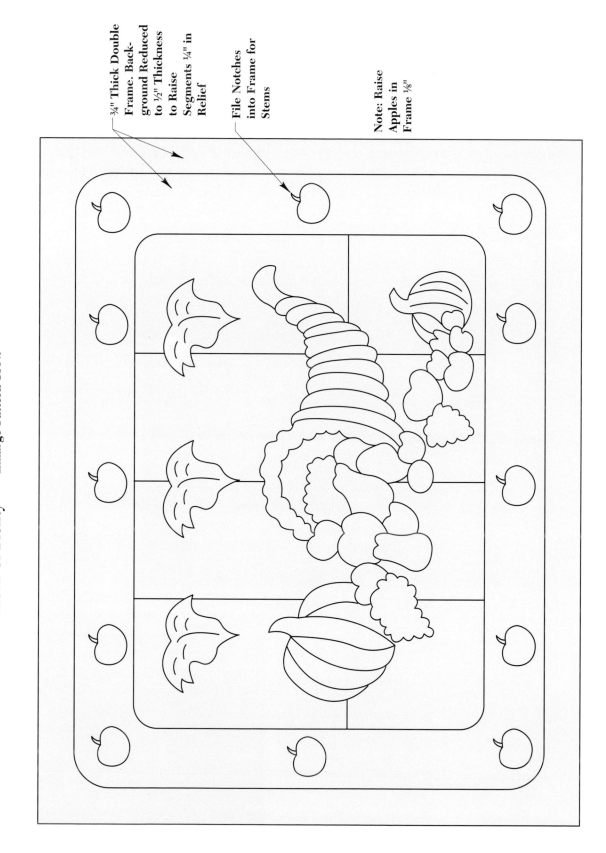

Horn of Plenty   Enlarge Pattern 130%

5–26. Use ¾ × 7⅜ × 9¼-inch solid wood and a ¼-inch plywood backer.

¾" Thick Double Frame. Back-ground Reduced to ½" Thickness to Raise Segments ¼" in Relief

File Notches into Frame for Stems

Note: Raise Apples in Frame ⅛"

Elf with Flowers

For this project (**5–27** to **5–31**), use ¾-inch solid wood and a ¼-inch backer, both cut to 8¾ × 11 inches. First cut the frame free and glue it to the backer with a sawn beveled edge all around. Next, cut out all of the segments (**5–29**); however, keep the six lower white pieces of the mushroom in one piece until after resawing it to thickness (**5–30**). Resaw the background pieces to remove ½ inch of material from their total thickness (**5–31**).

Prepare a ⅛-inch-thick shim to elevate the elf's right arm. Reduce the thicknesses of all the other segments as specified on the pattern. Round over and/or shape the segments. Paint and glue them to the backer.

5–27. Elf with Flowers has greatly reduced background segments and only the right arm is elevated with a ⅛-inch shim.

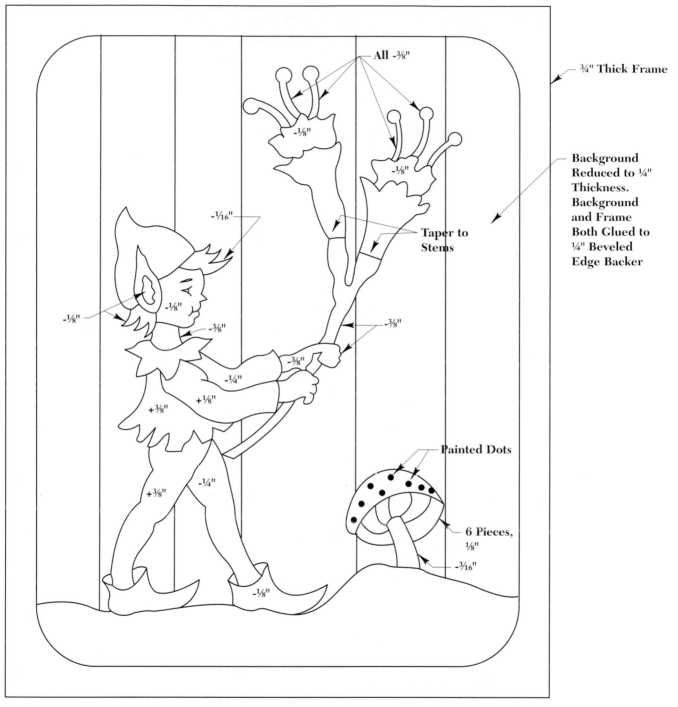

Elf with Flowers

Enlarge Pattern 155%

5–28. Use ¾ × 8¾ × 11-inch solid wood and a ¼-inch backer

5–29. Sawing out the segments.

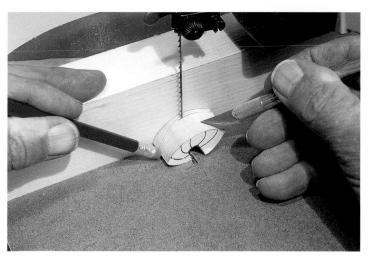

5–30. The lower mushroom pieces are all resawn to thickness at the same time before being cut into individual segments.

5–31. The background pieces are all resawn to remove ½ inch of their total thickness, leaving just ¼-inch material to be glued to the backer.

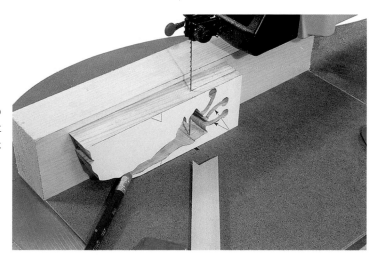

Cape Cod Lighthouse

This project (**5–32** and **5–33**) is made from two layers of plywood 8 inches square by ¼ inch or less in thickness. Approximately 30 linear inches of ¾-inch-square frame material is required. Cut both pieces of plywood to octagon shapes of the same size. Saw the segments from one of the pieces of plywood. Paint and glue them to the second piece of plywood (the backer) to make a regular flat project without any relief. Rabbet the frame stock. Rout or saw the chamfered edges and miter-cut them to length at 67½ degrees.

5–32. Cape Cod Lighthouse. This is simply a flat segmentation project made from plywood with a frame of solid wood.

5–33. Use plywood ¼ inch or less in thickness with approximately 30 linear inches of ¾-inch-square frame stock.

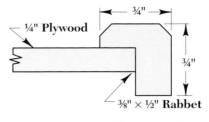

Frame Section
(Full Size)

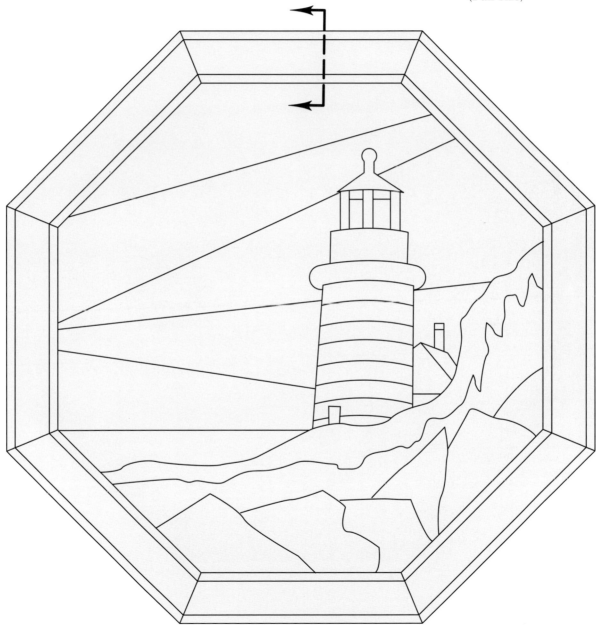

Cape Cod Lighthouse
Enlarge Pattern 140%

Abstraction

Abstraction (**5–34** and **5–35**) is made exactly like Cape Cod Lighthouse except all of the geometrical shapes are raised ⅛ inch in relief. This project requires two pieces of plywood that are 10⅜ inches square and ¼ inch or less in thickness and approximately 40 linear inches of ¾-inch-square solid-wood frame stock. The plywood background is sponge-painted blue over a base coat of white.

5–34. Abstraction is another project made from plywood ¼ inch or less in thickness, with a solid-wood frame.

5–35. Two pieces of plywood ¼ inch or less in thickness × 10⅜ inches square and approximately 40 linear inches of ¾-inch-square solid wood are required.

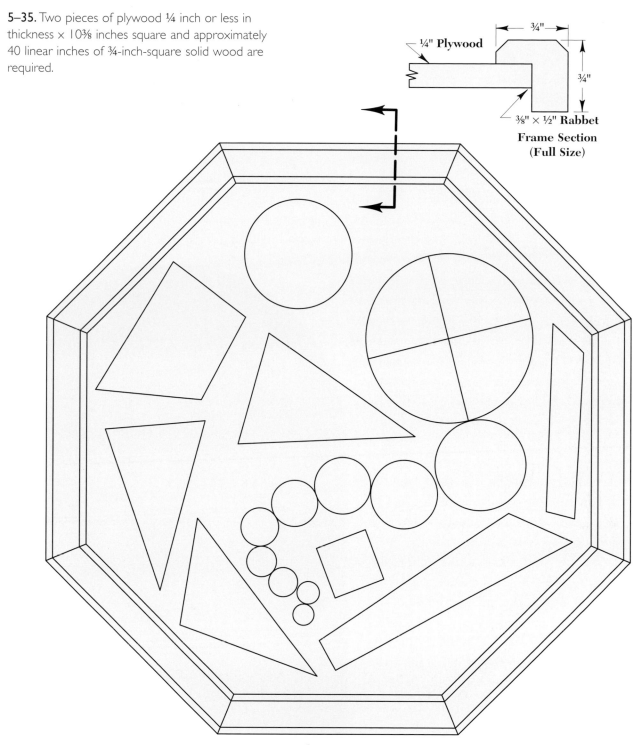

¼" Plywood

¾"

¾"

⅜" × ½" **Rabbet**

Frame Section
(Full Size)

Abstraction
Enlarge Pattern 180%

Castle

This classic project (**5–36** to **5–44**) is completely stain-finished and consists of a segmented castle overlay glued to a framed plywood plaque. The material requirements are:

1 piece of ½ × 6⅝ × 11⅛-inch plywood, for the plaque

1 piece of ⅛ or ¼ × 7⅝ × 12¼-inch plywood, for the backer

1 piece of ½ × ¾ × approximately 30-inch solid wood, for the straight frame stock

1 piece of ¾ × 4 × 7¾-inch solid wood, for sawn curved frame stock

1 piece of ¾ × 4¼ × 6⅜-inch solid wood, for the castle

1 piece of 1 × 1⅜" × 6½-inch solid wood, for the stone.

Section D-D of the pattern (**5–38**) shows that the ½-inch-thick plywood plaque actually sits inside the frame pieces. The frame pieces and the background plaque are both glued to a ⅛-inch plywood backer. This requires careful layout and cutting so that no gaps exist anywhere along the inside of the frame pieces.

Begin by cutting the large stone-line pieces that extend along the base of the castle from the piece of 1-inch-thick wood (**5–39** to **5–41**). Shape, stain, and glue–assemble the pieces as shown in **5–42**. Use this assembly to make a new bottom layout line, and cut on the bottom of the castle piece itself (**5–43**). This ensures a good fit.

Next, cut all around the outside profile of the castle. Saw out the cross and set it aside (**5–44**). The castle itself is first cut into essentially 14 horizontal layers. Each is then shaped using the scroll saw with a compound-sawing technique to round

and shape the front surface. Round over all horizontal edges to about a 1⁄16-inch radius.

Use a wood-burning tool or file to indicate the vertical separations of the stone-like blocks. Use the burning tool to also detail the door surface, which is set back approximately ⅛ inch below the level of the doorframe. Sand and stain all parts. Stain the framed plaque, but mask off the area for the castle. Finish and glue the segments onto the plaque. Finally, when everything is dry, apply a clear top coat.

5–36. Castle. The dark stain finish on this segmented project provides a classic medieval look.

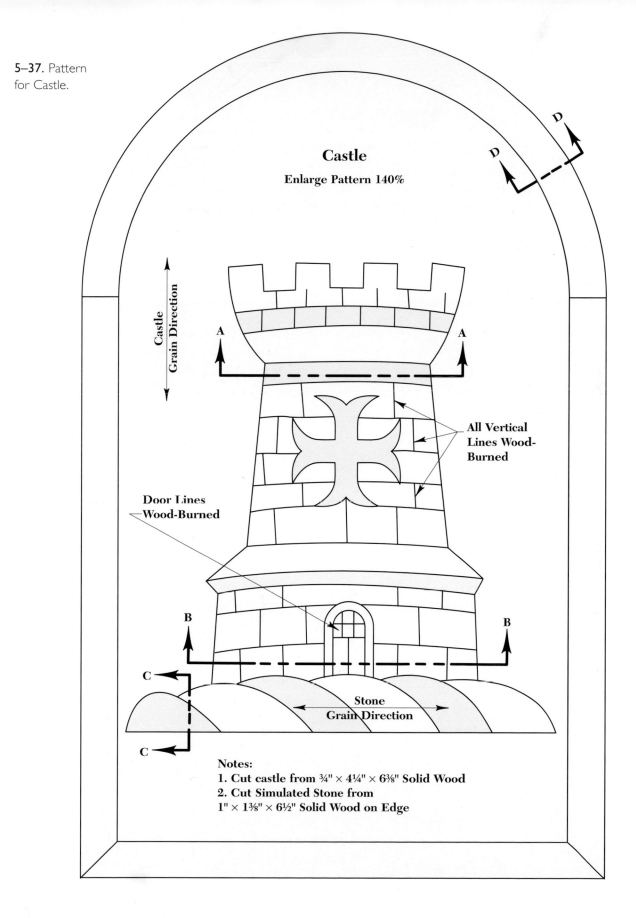

Castle

Enlarge Pattern 140%

D

D

Castle Grain Direction

A   A

All Vertical Lines Wood-Burned

Door Lines Wood-Burned

B   B

C

Stone Grain Direction

C

Notes:
1. Cut castle from ¾" × 4¼" × 6⅜" Solid Wood
2. Cut Simulated Stone from
1" × 1⅜" × 6½" Solid Wood on Edge

5–38. Full-size section views provide guides for shaping key contours and show essential assembly details.

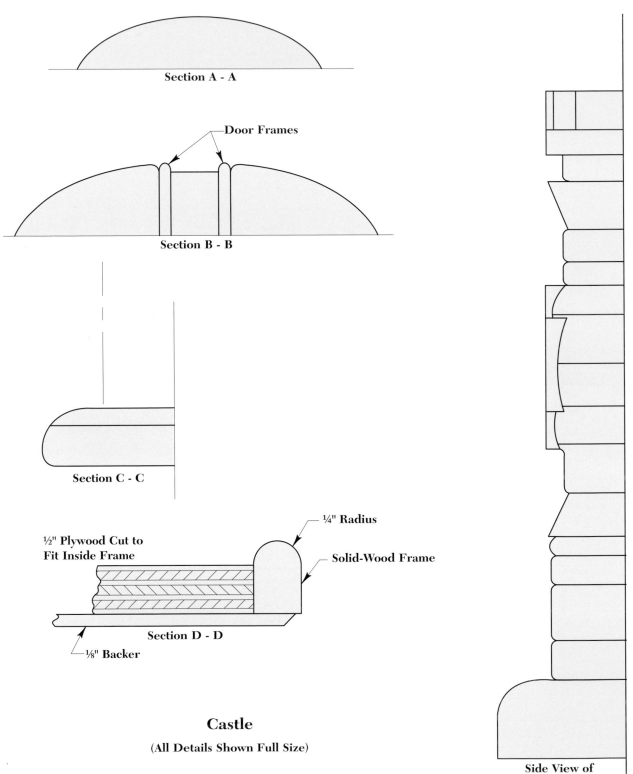

Section A - A

Door Frames

Section B - B

Section C - C

½" Plywood Cut to
Fit Inside Frame

¼" Radius

Solid-Wood Frame

Section D - D

⅛" Backer

Castle

(All Details Shown Full Size)

**Side View of
Segmented Overlay**

5–39. This closeup shows how the large stone-like base under the castle projects forward and extends to each side.

5–40. The "stones" are sawn from a strip of 1 x 1⅜-inch wood cut on its edge as shown.

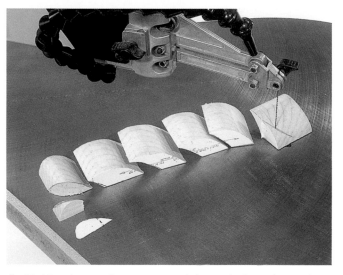

5–41. Use the scroll saw to round the end pieces by sawing them to a rough shape as shown.

5–42. Shape all six pieces and then stain alternate pieces but not the gluing surfaces. Glue the assembly together as shown.

5–43. Transfer the contour of the shaped and assembled stones to create an accurate cutting line along the base of the castle.

5–44. The base of the castle should sit on top of the stones as shown.

Chapter 6

Standing Projects

Featured in the chapter are a dozen projects incorporating fundamental segmentation techniques that are designed to stand up or sit upon a flat surface. The statuette projects look as if they were hand-carved. Some projects are unusual and just fun to make. A few projects are even functional with space for clock inserts. All projects are made from readily accessible material, most of which may be found in the scrap bin. Brief instructions and photos will clarify unusual techniques.

Haida Tribe Totem Pole. See pages 108 to 111 for project.

Bicycle Racer. See pages 88 and 89 for project.

Biker Doing Wheelie

This is a pretty basic project (**6–1** to **6–3**), with the segmentation work made from a piece of ¾ × 3 × 4¾-inch stock that is mounted to a ⅜ × 4¾ × 5½-inch plywood backer, with a ¾ × 1⅛ × 6¼-inch base. The thickest piece is the biker's hat, and all other pieces are reduced as indicated on the patterns (**6–2** and **6–3**).

The base and background finish is sponge-applied over a one-color base coat. The dots on the shirt are painted. Install a mini-clock or picture frame insert to complete the project.

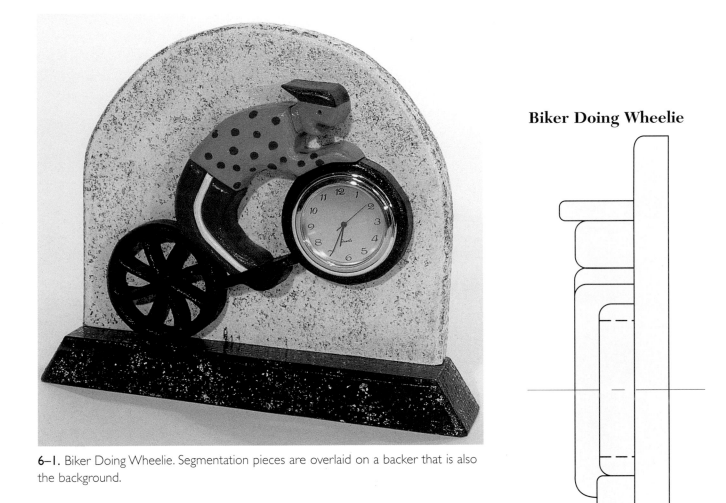

Biker Doing Wheelie

6–1. Biker Doing Wheelie. Segmentation pieces are overlaid on a backer that is also the background.

Glue

6–2. Side-view pattern, full-size.

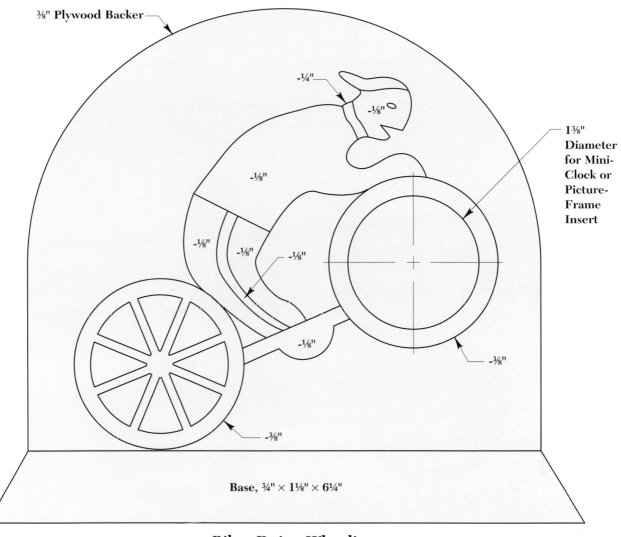

⅜" Plywood Backer

−¼"

−⅛"

1⅜" Diameter for Mini-Clock or Picture-Frame Insert

−⅛"

−⅛"

−⅛"

−⅛"

−⅛"

−⅜"

−⅜"

Base, ¾" × 1⅛" × 6¼"

Biker Doing Wheelie
Full-Size Pattern

6–3. Full-size pattern for Biker Doing Wheelie.

Bicycle Racer

The photo frame and clock insert make this project (**6–4** and **6–5**) the perfect desktop piece for the avid biker. The biker is made from ¾ × 3¼ × 5-inch solid stock and a backer of ⅛-inch plywood of the same size. The sizes for the two base pieces are ¾ × 2⅛ × 8 inches and ¾ × ¾ × 6¼ inches. The fractions on the pattern indicate the amount of material removed from the original ¾-inch thickness. Notice that the backer is visible through several openings from the front (**6–4**). This was done to give strength to the project. These areas are, however, painted black before assembly and hardly noticeable.

6–4. Bicycle Racer. This stand-up version is the same general design as the wall plaque project on pages 58 and 59. Here, however, a photo frame and a clock insert are set into the wheels.

6–5. Full-size pattern for Bicycle Racer. Notice the cutout areas revealing the painted surface of the backer.

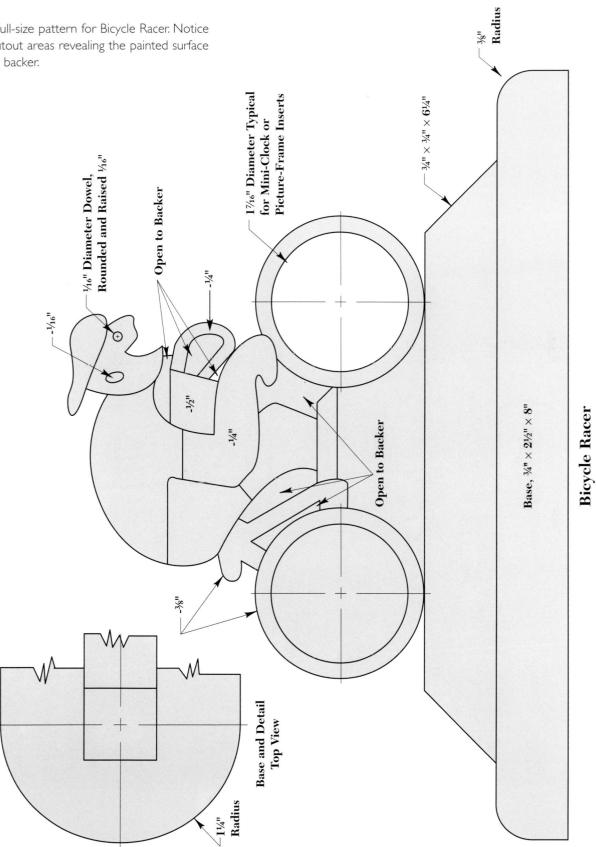

3/8" Radius

3/4" × 3/4" × 6¼"

1⁷/₁₆" Diameter Typical for Mini-Clock or Picture-Frame Inserts

1/16" Diameter Dowel, Rounded and Raised 1/16"

Open to Backer

Open to Backer

Open to Backer

−1/16"

−1/4"

−1/2"

−1/4"

−3/8"

Base, 3/4" × 2½" × 8"

Bicycle Racer
Full-Size Pattern

1¼" Radius

Base and Detail Top View

89

Grandma & Bicycle Clock

Like the Biker Doing Wheelie on pages 86 and 87, the segmented pieces of this project (**6–6** and **6–7**) are glued to a visible, sponge-painted backer. Grandma and her bike segments begin as a piece of ¾ × 5¼ × 5¼-inch solid wood. Various segments are resawn or reduced in thickness by removing the amount of mate-rial as specified on the pattern. The base "clouds" are cut from scraps or one ¾ × 1¼ × 6¼-inch piece with the center cloud reduced to a ⅜-inch thickness. The backer/background is ⅛ × 6¾ × 7½ inches and the base is ¾ × 1½ × 7½ inches. A close look at **6–6** shows some minor details of Grandma's dress painted in white.

6–6. Grandma & Bicycle Clock.

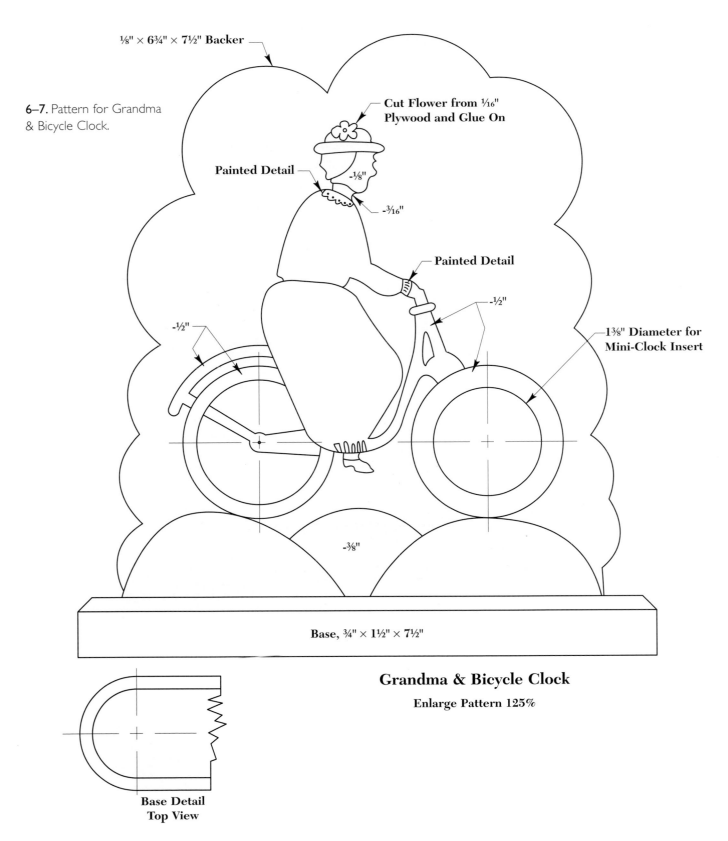

⅛" × 6¾" × 7½" Backer

6–7. Pattern for Grandma & Bicycle Clock.

Cut Flower from ¹⁄₁₆" Plywood and Glue On

Painted Detail

-⅛"

-³⁄₁₆"

Painted Detail

-½"

-½"

1⅜" Diameter for Mini-Clock Insert

-⅜"

Base, ¾" × 1½" × 7½"

Grandma & Bicycle Clock

Enlarge Pattern 125%

Base Detail
Top View

Amish Horse & Buggy Clock

This is another project (**6–8** to **6–10**) with essentially the same structural features as Biker Doing Wheelie and Grandma & Bicycle Clock. Other than the ⅛ × 5½ × 10-inch backer/background, all segments are sawn from ¾-inch thick stock: The man is ¾ × 1½ × 2 inches, the buggy is ¾ × 2 × 2½ inches, the horse is ¾ × 3⅜ × 5 inches, and the two base pieces are ½ × ¾ × 7¾ inches and ¾ × 2 × 10⅜ inches. Glue or a clear acrylic spray finish will stiffen the strings (reins). The strings run through holes drilled in the backer and are knotted and glued down on the rear side. The end of the rein runs through a hole drilled through the driver's hand. Small dots of paint highlight the eyes of the horse and the man.

6–8. Amish Horse & Buggy Clock.

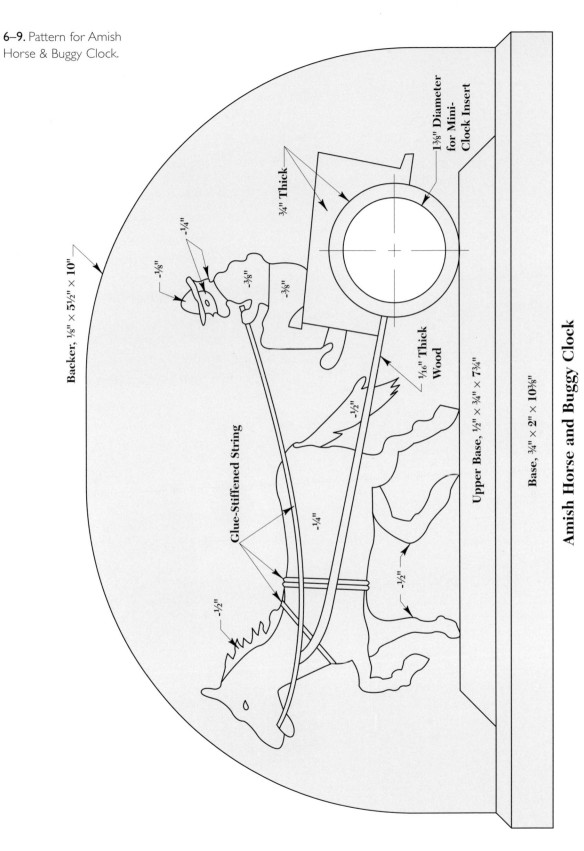

Backer, ⅛" × 5½" × 10"

−¼"

−⅛"

−⅜"

−⅜"

¾" Thick

1⅜" Diameter
for Mini-
Clock Insert

Glue-Stiffened String

−½"

−¼"

−½"

−½"

¹⁄₁₆" Thick
Wood

Upper Base, ½" × ¾" × 7¾"

Base, ¾" × 2" × 10⅜"

Amish Horse and Buggy Clock
Enlarge Pattern 125%

Amish Horse and Buggy Clock

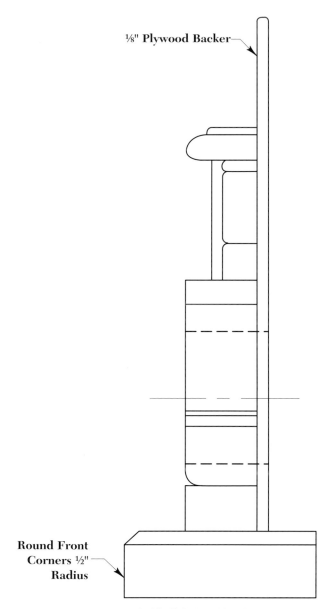

⅛" Plywood Backer

Round Front
Corners ½"
Radius

6–10. Full-size side-view pattern.

Birthday Girl

This is an interesting project in that segments for the eyes, nose, and cheeks are cut out and rounded over (**6–11** to **6–15**). The girl is made from one ¾ × 3¾ × 5¼-inch piece with an ⅛-inch-thick backer the same size. The piece she sits on is ¾ × 1¾ × 2 inches, and the base piece is ¾ × 2¼ × 7¾ inches.

Begin by making the girl as a separate project with its own backer. The nose, cheeks, and eyes are very small pieces with rounded surfaces. The surrounding face area is reduced ⅛ inch in thickness. Her feet are shimmed out ¼ inch with small pieces of plywood. The balloons are rounded ⅜-inch stock and supported with painted wire.

The rear surfaces of the backer and the part the girl sits on are set flush on the rear side so the girl is actually forward ⅛ inch in relief (**6–14** and **6–15**).

6–11. Birthday Girl.

94

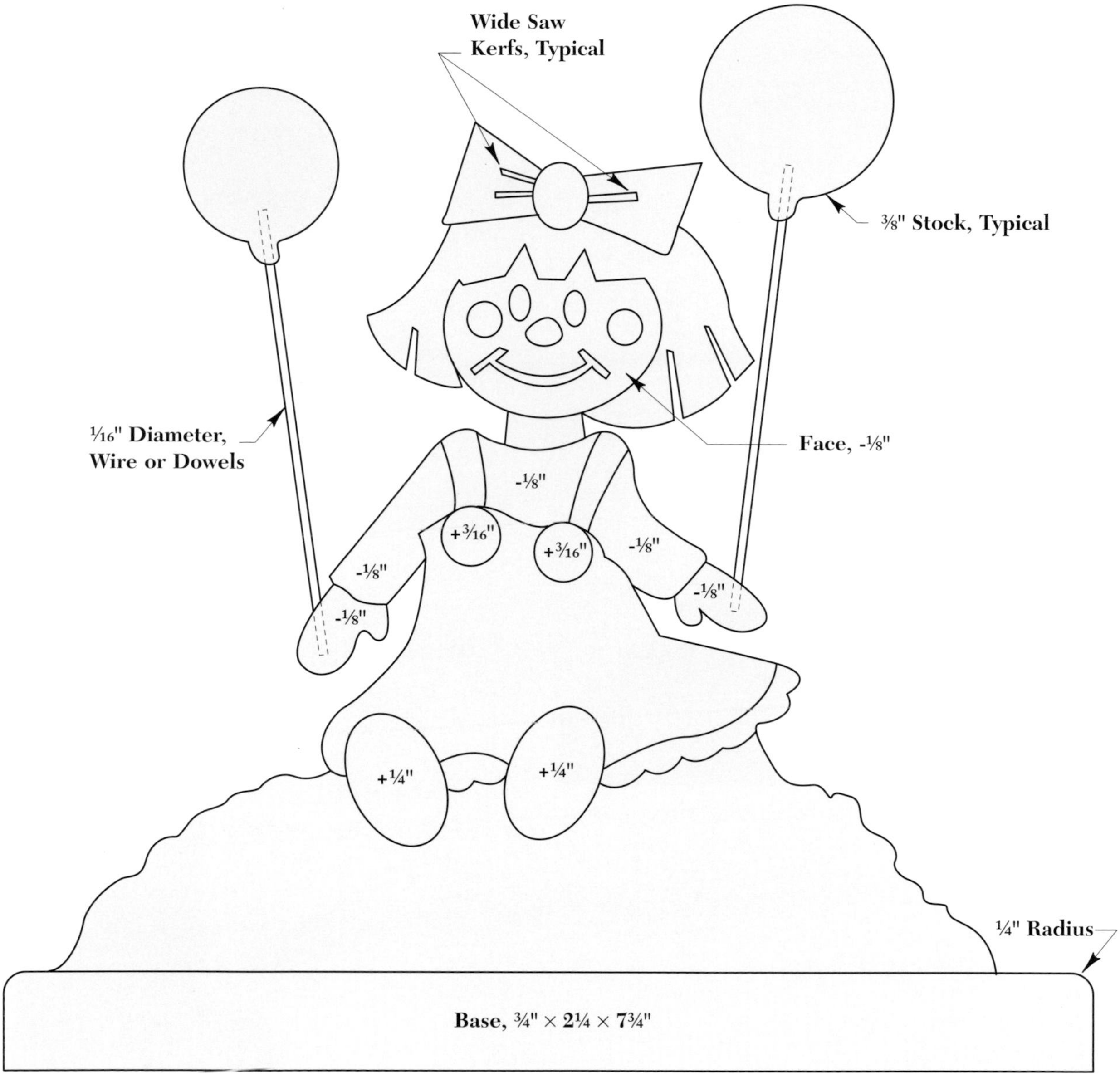
Wide Saw
Kerfs, Typical
3/8" Stock, Typical
1/16" Diameter,
Wire or Dowels
Face, -1/8"
-1/8"
+3/16"
+3/16"
-1/8"
-1/8"
-1/8"
-1/8"
+1/4"
+1/4"
1/4" Radius
Base, 3/4" × 2 1/4 × 7 3/4"

Birthday Girl

Enlarge Pattern 125%

6–12. Pattern for Birthday Girl.

6–13. This closeup of Birthday Girl shows how nicely a No. 2 blade cuts out the face segments and how all pieces are shaped.

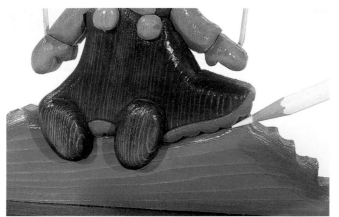

6–14. The girl is made as a separate segmentation project with a typical backer of ⅛-inch plywood. Then it is glued to the light-green base piece, but set forward ⅛ inch.

6–15. This side-view photo shows the backer and how the girl is set forward ⅛ inch on the piece she sits on.

Hawaiian War God

Here's a quick and fun-to-make statuette with character that's also useful (**6–16** to **6–19**). Begin with one piece of ¾ × 3½× 10¾-inch solid wood and a ⅛-inch plywood backer the same size. Illus. **6–19** provides a full-size pattern for the ¾ × 3½ × 5¾-inch base.

Saw out all of the segments and note, however, that there are many open areas (without segments) that expose the surface of a black-painted backer. The various segments of the face are shaped or rounded over and set forward in relief with shims. The nose requires a little creative shaping; its lower edge and the inside edges of the mouth and teeth are not rounded.

Just the two stains create a very effective look. Top off with a clear acrylic finish.

6–16. Hawaiian War God.

6–17. This closeup shows one of the many open areas of the project that are visible to painted areas of the ⅛-inch-thick plywood backer. Notice that the many face segments are set forward in relief, as are the feet.

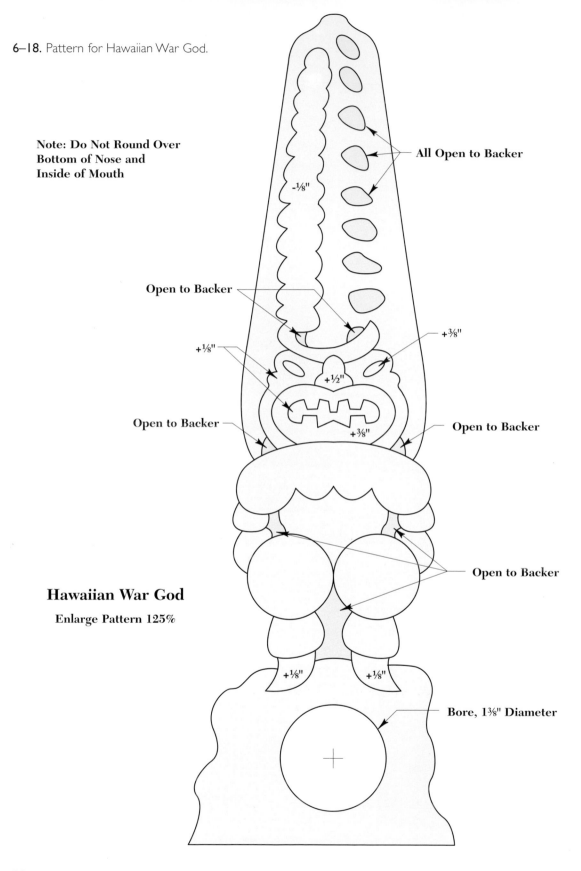

**Note: Do Not Round Over
Bottom of Nose and
Inside of Mouth**

All Open to Backer

Open to Backer

+⅜"

+⅛"

+½"

Open to Backer

Open to Backer

+⅜"

Hawaiian War God

Enlarge Pattern 125%

Open to Backer

+⅛"   +⅛"

Bore, 1⅜" Diameter

-⅛"

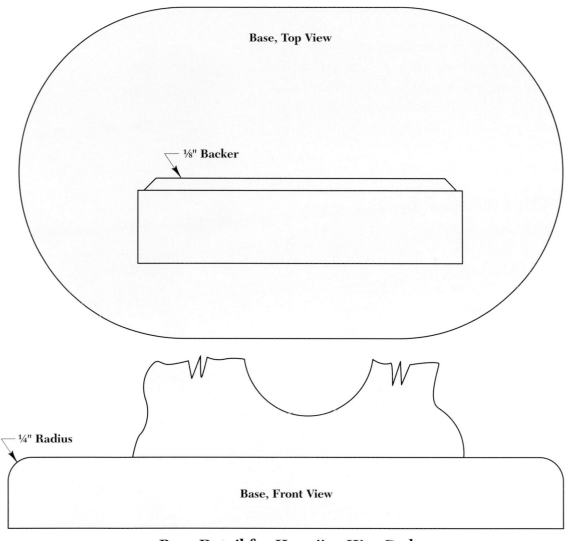

Base, Top View

⅛" Backer

¼" Radius

Base, Front View

Base Detail for Hawaiian War God

Full-size Patterns

6–19. Full-size top and front views of the base and assembly detail for the Hawaiian War God.

Kachina Doll

This sculpture (**6–20** to **6–25**) combines straight and bevel scroll-sawing plus basic segmentation techniques to create a project that looks as if it were completely hand-carved. Very little carving is actually required. Use ¾-inch-thick softwood scraps and a piece of ⅛ × 1½ × 3⅜-inch solid-wood material for a backer. Feathers can be purchased at your local craft shop or Wal-Mart.

The body consists of three individual blocks, all with vertical grain. Apply the patterns and cut out the internal segments. Round over the outside edges to almost a ¾-inch radius (**6–22**). Set the table saw to 15 degrees and bevel-saw the legs. Bevel-saw the 2½-inch-diameter base at 30 degrees (**6–23**). Paint all surfaces except those areas to be glued. The headpiece and horns are glued and also fastened with small brads used as dowels as shown on the pattern (**6–21**). Note in **6–24** how some segments are set back, set forward, or remain flush. Illus. **6–25** shows how the solid-wood backer is shaped with a ⅛-inch radius and painted.

6–20. Kachina Doll looks like it was all hand-carved, but in fact very little carving is involved at all.

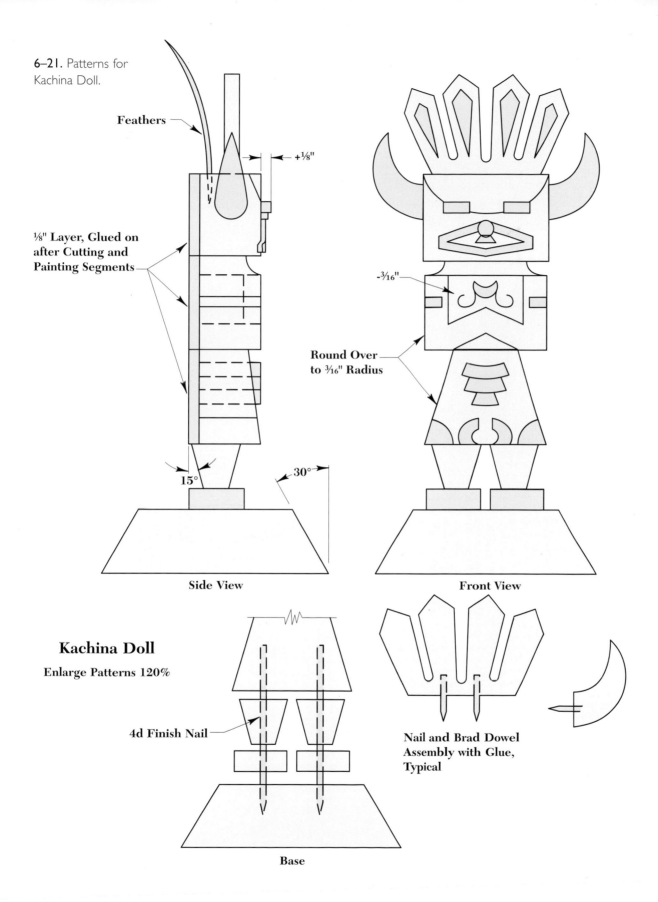

6–21. Patterns for Kachina Doll.

Feathers

+⅛"

⅛" Layer, Glued on after Cutting and Painting Segments

-³⁄₁₆"

Round Over to ³⁄₁₆" Radius

15°

30°

Side View

Front View

Kachina Doll

Enlarge Patterns 120%

4d Finish Nail

Base

Nail and Brad Dowel Assembly with Glue, Typical

6–22. Rounding over the front contours of the lower body piece. Use a knife as shown or a rotary tool.

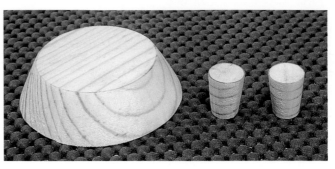

6–23. The base and leg pieces are bevel-sawn.

6–24. This closeup shows segments that are set back (reduced), set forward, or set flush to the surface.

6–25. The backer edges are shaped to match and painted because they are visible from the side.

"Totem Pole & Tepee"

The Totem Pole & Tepee (**6–26** to **6–36**), like the Kachina Doll, is a clever scroll-sawn project of table art that at first glance appears to be hand-carved. The tepee (**6–36**) is merely an option to make if desired and is discussed on page 105. Other than simple rounding over, very little carving or shaping is involved. The edges of the scroll-sawn cut-out segments are rounded over, painted, reinserted into their original cavities, and then glued in place. Some segments are glued so their face surfaces are ⅛ to ½ inch above the surrounding background (**6–27**).

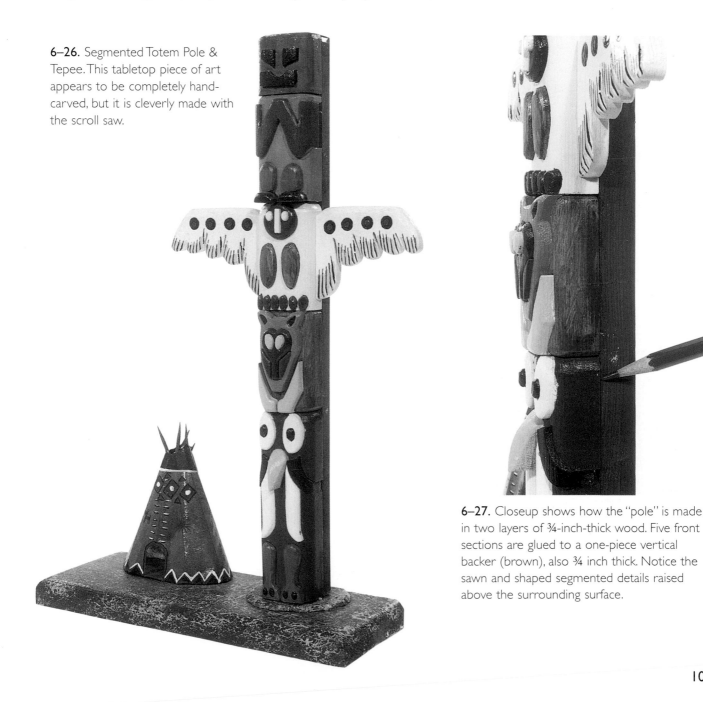

6–26. Segmented Totem Pole & Tepee. This tabletop piece of art appears to be completely hand-carved, but it is cleverly made with the scroll saw.

6–27. Closeup shows how the "pole" is made in two layers of ¾-inch-thick wood. Five front sections are glued to a one-piece vertical backer (brown), also ¾ inch thick. Notice the sawn and shaped segmented details raised above the surrounding surface.

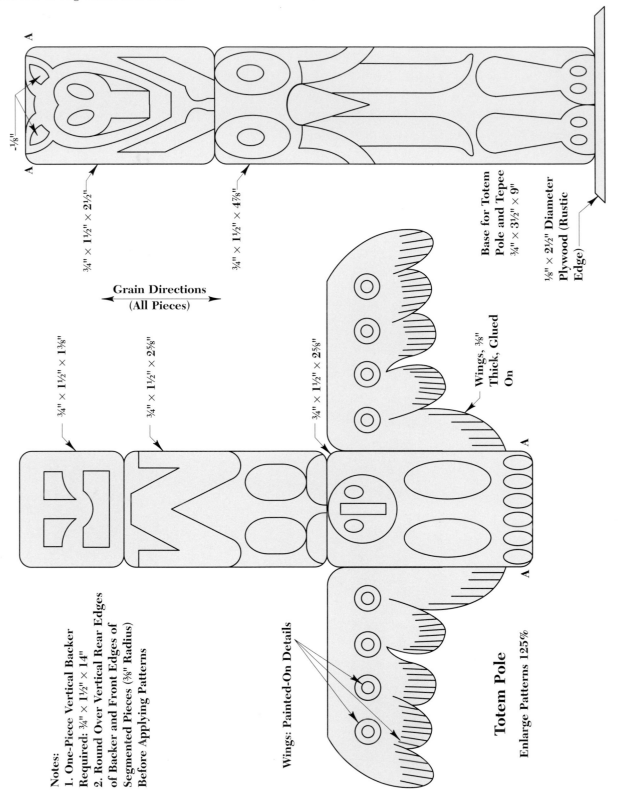

−⅛"

¾" × 1½" × 2½"

¾" × 1½" × 4⅞"

Grain Directions
(All Pieces)

¾" × 1½" × 1⅜"

¾" × 1½" × 2⅝"

¾" × 1½" × 2⅝"

Base for Totem Pole and Tepee
¾" × 3½" × 9"

⅛" × 2½" Diameter Plywood (Rustic Edge)

Wings, ⅜" Thick, Glued On

Notes:
1. One-Piece Vertical Backer
Required: ¾" × 1½" × 14"
2. Round Over Vertical Rear Edges of Backer and Front Edges of Segmented Pieces (⅜" Radius) Before Applying Patterns

Wings: Painted-On Details

Totem Pole
Enlarge Patterns 125%

The totem pole is made from five segmented sections of softwood ¾ × 1½ inches in width and of various lengths that are eventually glued to a one-piece backer that is ¾ × 1½ × 14 inches. Use a router (optional) to round over the vertical edges of the front sections before cutting them to length (**6–29**). Now, after the edges have been rounded over, apply the cutting patterns. Notice that the wings have vertical grain direction and are cut from ⅜-inch material.

Use a No. 2 or 2/0 blade and saw out all of the segments. Notice that some cuts can be made by sawing inward from the outside edges. Some cuts, however, require blade-threading holes (1/32 inch in diameter) (**6–30** to **6–32**). Paint all nonglued surfaces

6–30. Drill 1/32-inch-diameter entry holes at the lower edges of the inside segments as shown here in the eyes and inside ear pieces.

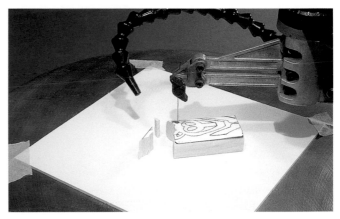

6–31. The small pieces sawn free remain supported when using the aid of an auxiliary table with a zero blade-clearance hole.

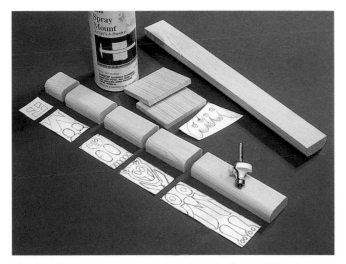

6–29. All pieces are prepared and ready for applying the individual patterns. Notice that the front vertical edges and the rear edges of the backer were rounded over with a ⅜-inch roundover router bit.

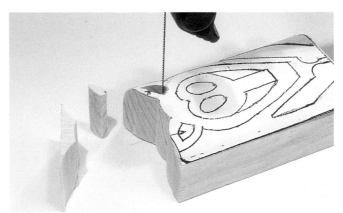

6–32. A closeup. Notice that the pattern was applied after the vertical edges were rounded over.

as per the colors shown in the various photos. Glue each of the five sections to the backer (**6–33** and **6–34**). Notice that the wings and some areas have simple painted details.

The painted and assembled totem pole can be mounted to the base with a dowel. The size and base details are given in **6–35**.

The tepee (**6–35**) is an optional addition. Use the full-size layout given on the pattern and cut it from heavy brown tagboard or a paper grocery bag. Shape it into a cone and glue it together. A coat of varnish will stiffen the paper. Decorate the tepee with hand-painted designs using those shown in **6–35** and **6–36** for reference.

6–33. This closeup shows the shaping and projection positions of the various segments. Notice that the interior segments of the ears are not shaped, but reduced in thickness and set below the surface. Conversely, the yellow nose projects almost ½ inch.

6–34. Elevating this segment creates a gap between it and the backer. Cut small scraps to fill this space.

6–35. The tepee (optional) is made from brown paper and varnished to stiffen it and create a hide-like look.

6–36. Base details and tepee pattern layout.

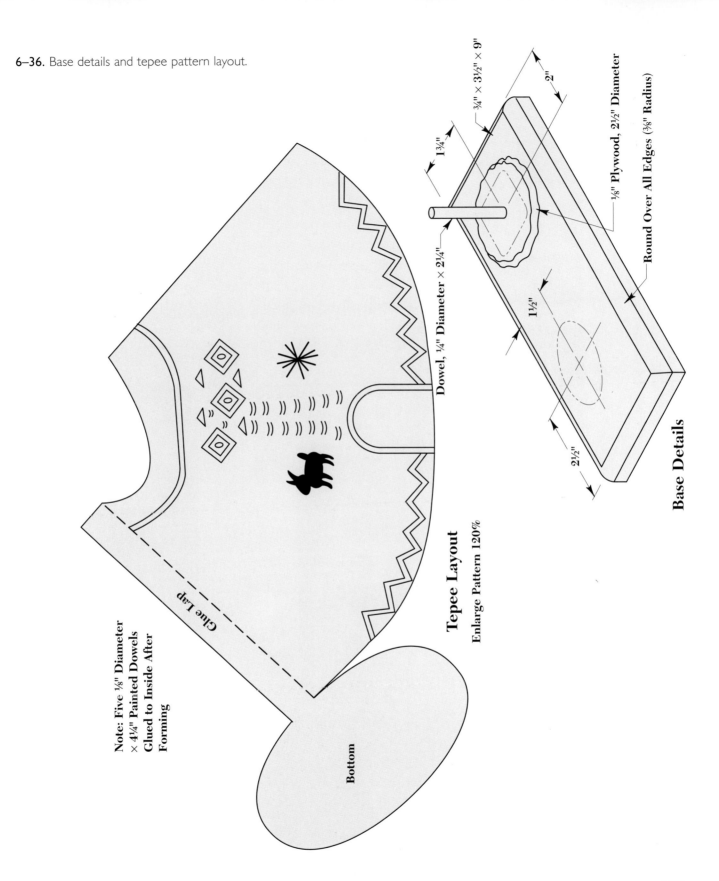

Note: Five ⅛" Diameter × 4¼" Painted Dowels Glued to Inside After Forming

Glue Lap

Bottom

Tepee Layout
Enlarge Pattern 120%

Dowel, ¼" Diameter × 2¼"

¾" × 3½" × 9"

2"

1¾"

1½"

2½"

⅛" Plywood, 2½" Diameter

Round Over All Edges (⅜" Radius)

Base Details

Haida Tribe Totem Pole

This project (**6–37** to **6–42**) is made essentially the same way as the totem pole described in Totem Pole & Tepee. Although larger, it is somewhat easier to make. The patterns are provided full-size and they give all of the essential dimensions and construction details. Study the side views of the patterns, as they indicate the amount of projection for the various segments and indicate shaping requirements. Illus. **6–38** and **6–39** show that none of the edges on the segments projected or raised above the surrounding surfaces are rounded over. They are actually left square as shown. Notice also that just one tongue and three noses have simple slanted or tapered surfaces. Some segments and the wings have some minor painted details, but these are relatively easy to duplicate using the photos for reference.

6–37.
Haida Tribe Totem Pole.

6–38. Closeup showing segmentation and painted details for the two top sections.

6–39. This closeup shows some detail in the middle and lower sections. Notice that the edges of the elevated inside cutout segments are not rounded over.

6—40. Patterns for the top sections for the Haida Tribe Totem Pole.

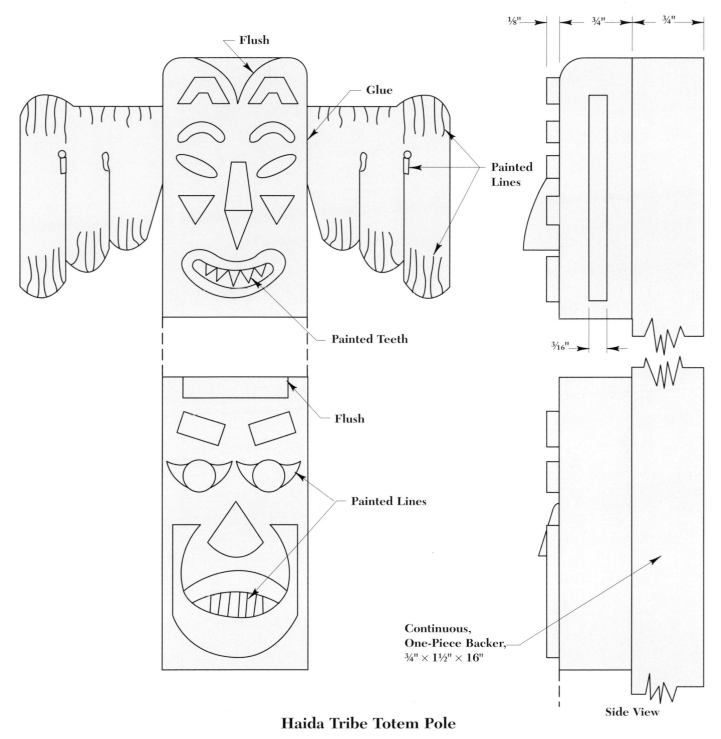

Haida Tribe Totem Pole

Full-Size Patterns

Patterns for
the middle
sections for
the Haida
Tribe Totem
Pole.

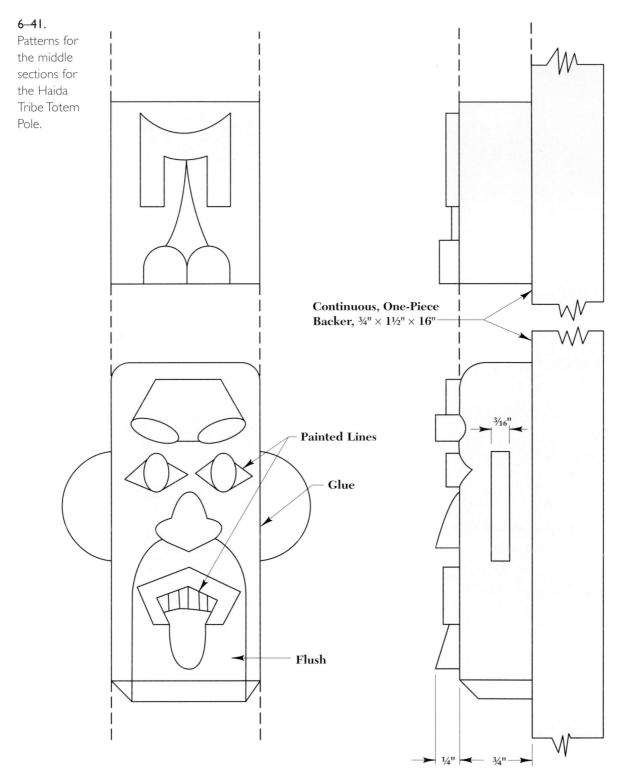

Continuous, One-Piece
Backer, ¾" × 1½" × 16"

Painted Lines

Glue

Flush

3/16"

¼"   ¾"

Haida Tribe Totem Pole

Full-Size Patterns

6–42. Patterns for the lower sections for the Haida Tribe Totem Pole.

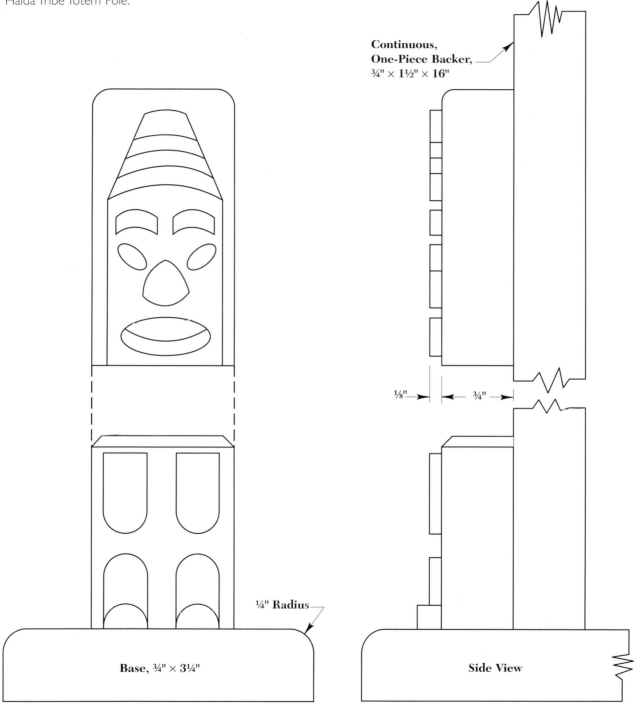

Continuous, One-Piece Backer, ¾" × 1½" × 16"

⅛"

¾"

¼" Radius

Base, ¾" × 3¼"

Side View

Haida Tribe Totem Pole

Full-Size Patterns

6–43. Chinese Monster Head.

Chinese Monster Head

This representation of a mythical creature dating to the 4th century B.C. (**6–43** to **6–46**) involves very elementary segmentation techniques coupled with some basic 3-D carving. The head and base are made from ¾ × 1¾ × 5-inch softwood, with a ⅛-inch solid-wood backer of the same size. The heavy base is 1¾ × 2⅝ × 3¼ inches. Refer to **6–44** and **6–46** for shaping of the segmented elements. The antlerlike horns are cut out separately from ⅜-inch solid wood and shaped, fitted, and glued to the head with instant or epoxy adhesive (**6–46**).

6–44. The ⅛-inch solid-wood backer is rounded and contoured as a visible part of the sculpture.

6–45. This closeup shows the lowered surfaces of the eyes and mouth. Notice the crooked nose.

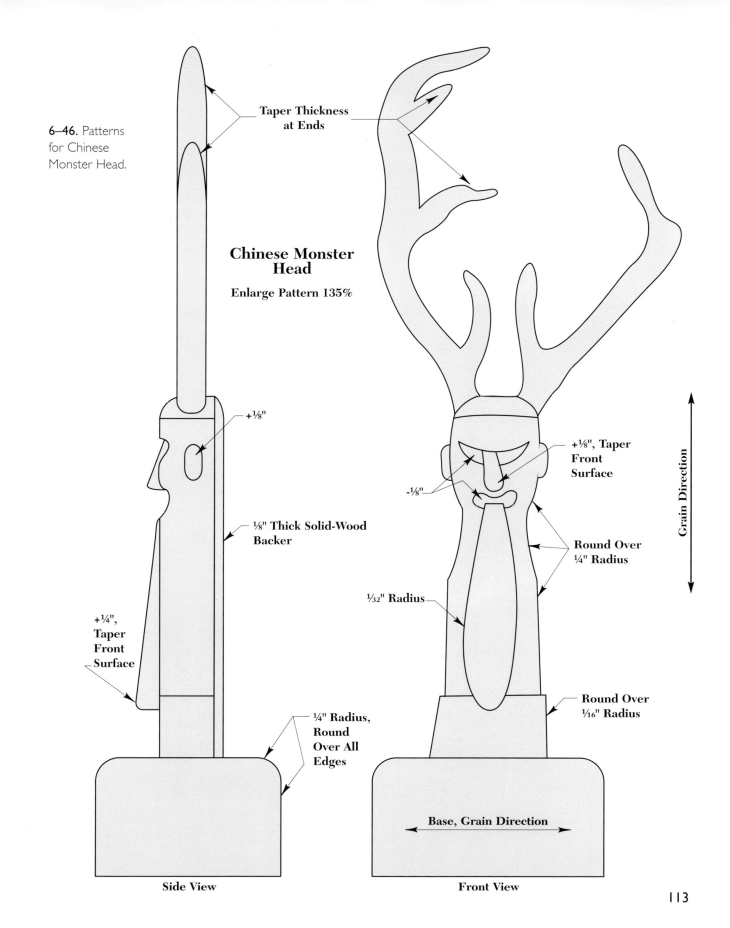

6–46. Patterns for Chinese Monster Head.

Taper Thickness at Ends

Chinese Monster Head

Enlarge Pattern 135%

+⅛"

⅛" Thick Solid-Wood Backer

+¼", Taper Front Surface

¼" Radius, Round Over All Edges

Side View

+⅛", Taper Front Surface

-⅛"

Round Over ¼" Radius

1/32" Radius

Round Over 1/16" Radius

Grain Direction

Base, Grain Direction

Front View

113

Hopi Kachina Doll Family

This project (**6–47** to **6–59**) involves creating three relatively simple crude-looking sculptures mounted onto a common base. The doll bodies are all made from ¾-inch solid wood and glued to a ¼-inch solid-wood backer (**6–48**). The bodies without arms are compound-sawn to include their legs, and each is made from one piece of wood (**6–52** to **6–56**). Illus. **6–57** to **6–59** show and describe essential shaping techniques involved in making each of the three sculptures.

The arms are sawn from individual pieces of scrap wood. Then they are shaped, fit, and glued to their respective bodies. Small pieces of denim or other fabric are glued to the finished bodies with a wrap of heavy string to simulate rope. Notice the feather on one doll, which can be obtained at a craft store or Wal-Mart.

The three figures are attached to a ¾ × 3½ × 9¾-inch base, with glue and small brads used as metal dowels (refer to **6–48**).

6–47. Hopi Kachina Doll Family.

6–48. Side view shows ¼-inch solid-wood backer and small brads used as dowels to attach the statuette to the base.

6–49. Patterns and base detail for Hopi Kachina Doll Family.

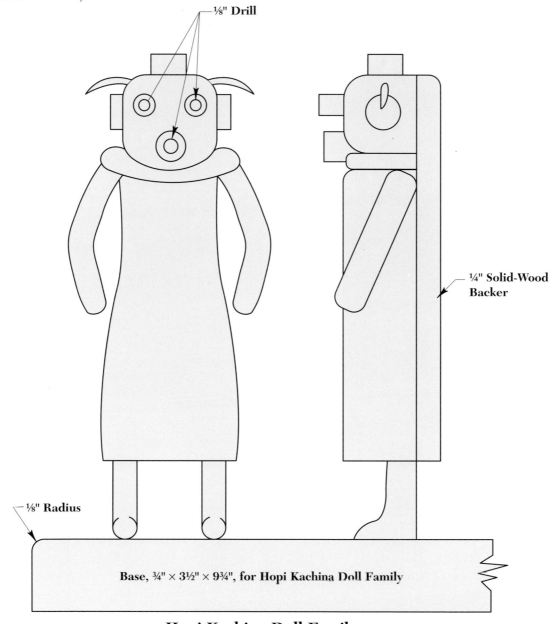

⅛" Drill

¼" Solid-Wood Backer

⅛" Radius

Base, ¾" × 3½" × 9¾", for Hopi Kachina Doll Family

Hopi Kachina Doll Family

Full-Size Patterns

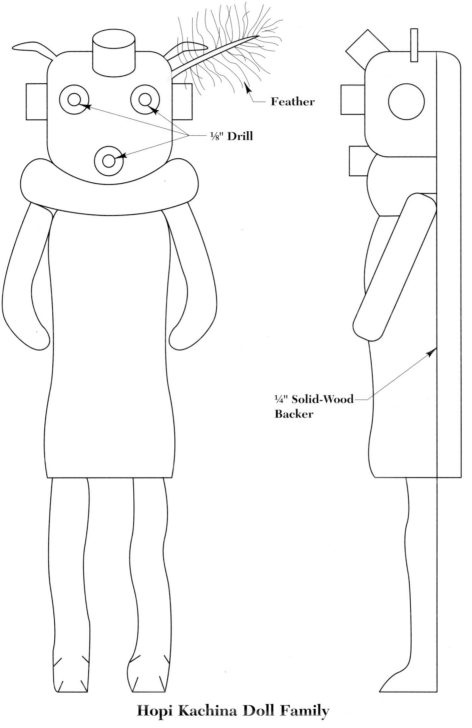

Feather

⅛" **Drill**

¼" **Solid-Wood
Backer**

Hopi Kachina Doll Family
Full-Size Patterns

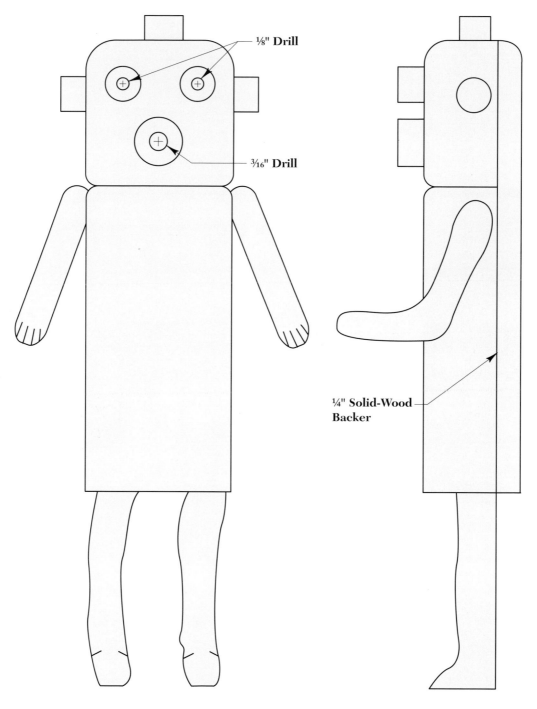

¹⁄₈" **Drill**

³⁄₁₆" **Drill**

¼" **Solid-Wood
Backer**

Hopi Kachina Doll Family
Full-Size Patterns

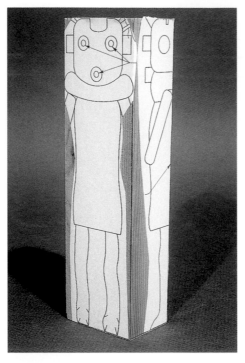

6–52. Patterns are applied to two adjoining surfaces of a ¾-inch-thick workpiece.

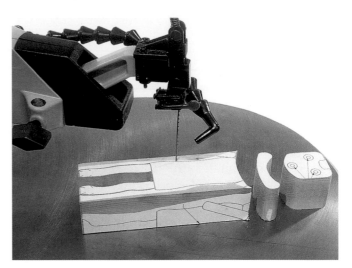

6–53. The head and collar pieces are cut free and set aside. Here the front-view body profile is being cut from the front-view pattern.

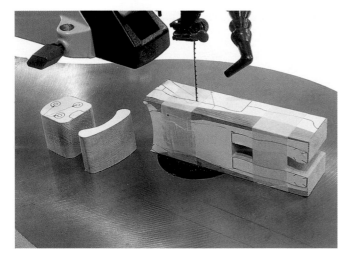

6–54. The side-view body profile is being cut next, with the waste pieces from the front view cuts replaced for support with wraps of masking tape.

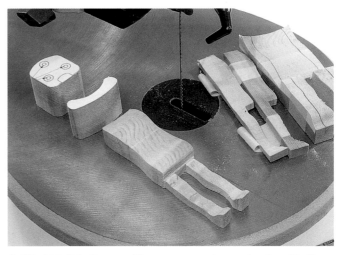

6–55. At left is the resulting compound-sawn body, with the waste pieces shown at the right.

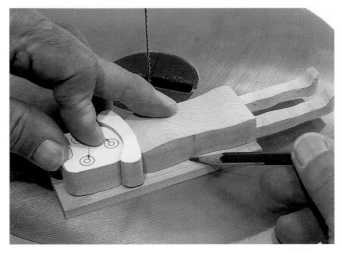

6–56. Tracing to provide a cutting line on the ¼-inch-thick solid-wood backer.

6–57. The cylindrical eyes and mouth pieces are cut out with the scroll saw. The ear pieces are ⅜-inch-diameter dowels or plug-like pieces made with a plug cutter.

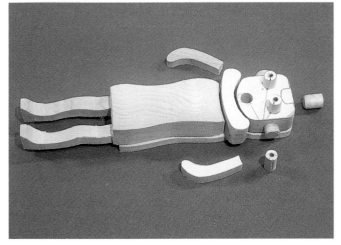

6–58. All pieces cut and ready for shaping.

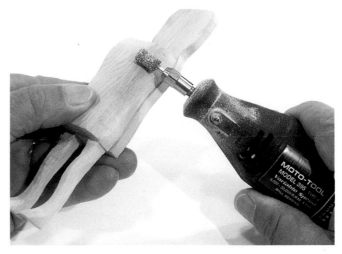

6–59. The body being shaped with a rotary tool and structured carbide cutter.

Knight in Armor

Making this project (**6–60** to **6–72**) involves basic segmentation skills, some compound-sawing, and a little tricky 3-D carving to shape the knight's right arm. Select one piece of ¾ × 2¾ × 8½-inch softwood to cut out the body pattern without the arms. A plywood backer measuring ⅛ × 2¾ × 8½ inches is also required. Various other pieces and the base are all small and stock can probably be found in the scrap bin. The necessary sizes are given in **6–62** and **6–63**.

Make the body, base, shield, and weapon parts first, employing basic woodworking and segmentation techniques. Notice how the segments all have rounded edges except the headpiece. This has two eye slots and a series of small holes that are open to the backer.

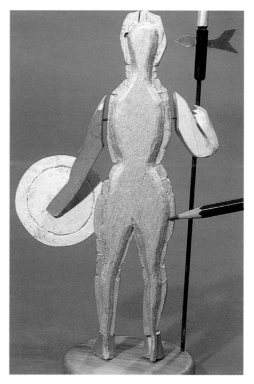

6–61. Rear view shows that the backer is generally not visible from the front or even at a three-quarter side view.

6–60. Knight in Armor. This project involves basic segmentation, some compound-sawing, and some basic 3-D carving techniques to shape the knight's right arm.

120

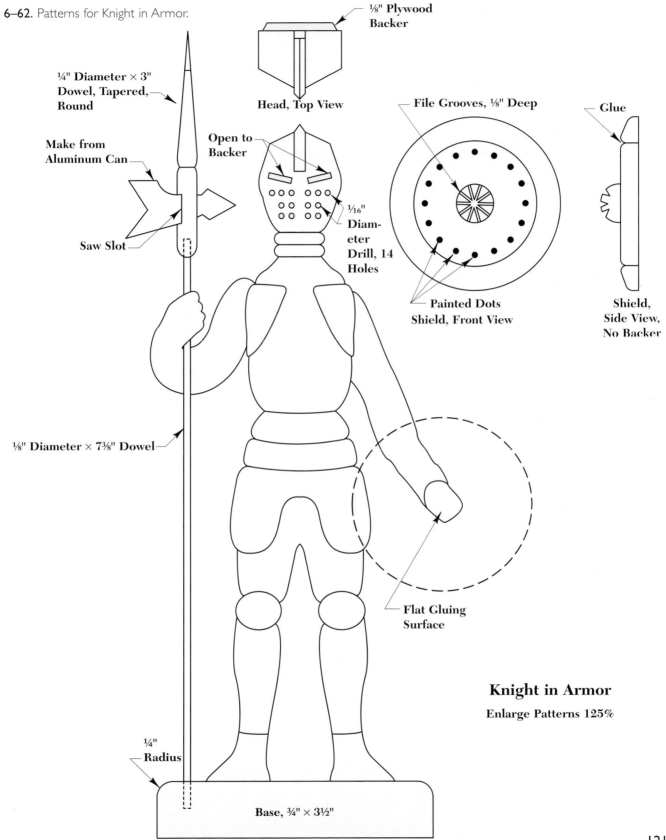

6–62. Patterns for Knight in Armor.

¼" Diameter × 3"
Dowel, Tapered,
Round

Make from
Aluminum Can

Saw Slot

⅛" Diameter × 7⅜" Dowel

¼"
Radius

⅛" Plywood
Backer

Head, Top View

Open to
Backer

1/16"
Diam-
eter
Drill, 14
Holes

File Grooves, ⅛" Deep

Painted Dots
Shield, Front View

Glue

Shield,
Side View,
No Backer

Flat Gluing
Surface

Base, ¾" × 3½"

Knight in Armor

Enlarge Patterns 125%

121

6–63. Patterns for Knight in Armor.

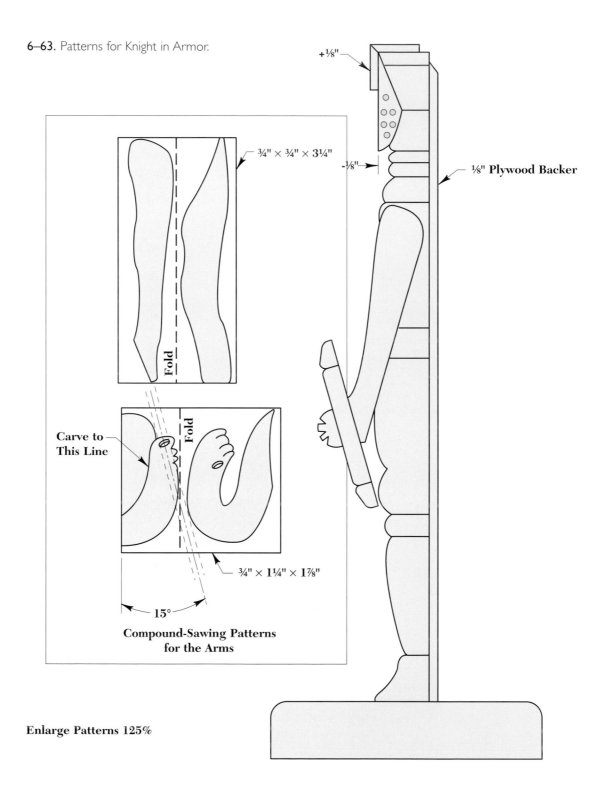

¾" × ¾" × 3¼"

Fold

Carve to
This Line

Fold

¾" × 1¼" × 1⅞"

15°

**Compound-Sawing Patterns
for the Arms**

Enlarge Patterns 125%

+⅛"

−⅛"

⅛" **Plywood Backer**

The arms are shaped by employing compound scroll-sawing techniques. Illus. **6–64** to **6–66** show closeups of the right arm as seen from several different positions. The compound-sawing patterns are given in **6–63**. Compound-sawing is the easiest way to rough out the shapes of the arms, especially the knight's right arm. Illus. **6–67** to **6–72** show and describe the procedure.

The dowel for the weapon should be close to vertical when viewed from the front and from the side. Drill ⁹⁄₆₄-inch holes through the left hand and into the base for the ⅛-inch-diameter dowel of the weapon. Hold the arm so that a line from the back of the shoulder to the elbow is about 12 to 15 degrees from vertical. Then drill the hole freehand, keeping the bit as vertical as possible. Insert the dowel through the hand, extending it to the base to locate the spot for the hole in the base.

The finish is simply a combination of basic aluminum spray paint and black paint. Paint the black accents on the shield, headpiece, and along the joint lines between segments. The black shading seen between the segments was applied using a finger after the segments were individually coated with aluminum paint.

6–64. The arms are cut to fit against the body. They are assembled with small brad (nail) dowels and glued. Notice that no finish is applied to the gluing areas.

6–65. Closeup of front view.

6–66. Closeup of left side view.

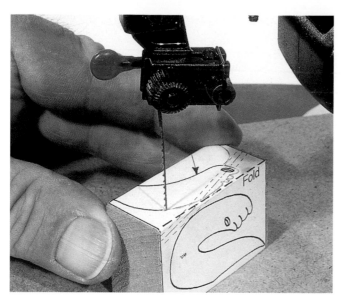

6–67. Pattern(s) applied to both surfaces. The first cut is shown in progress with the stock on its edge.

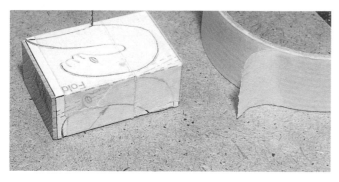

6–68. With the sawn waste pieces taped back to form the original block, the second pattern profile is cut out. Notice that the stock is now positioned on its larger, flat surface to make this cut.

6–69. The compound-sawn arm is shown completed at the right with the remaining scraps at its left.

6–70. Left side views of the compound-sawn blank compared to a completed arm sample at the right. Here a pencil line indicates stock that must still be removed.

6–71. Views of left arms as seen from the right side of the project. Another pencil line shows stock to be removed from the compound sawn blank to shape it like that of the completed carved arm sample shown at the right.

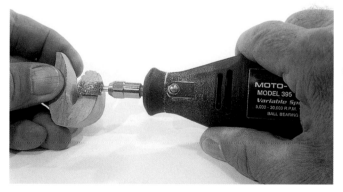

6–72. Holding the arm, as seen from a back view, while excess material is being removed with a rotary tool.

METRIC EQUIVALENCY CHART

Inches to Millimeters and Centimeters

MM=Millimeters   **CM=Centimeters**

Inches	MM	CM	Inches	CM	Inches	CM
⅛	3	0.3	9	22.9	30	76.2
¼	6	0.6	10	25.4	31	78.7
⅜	10	1.0	11	27.9	32	81.3
½	13	1.3	12	30.5	33	83.8
⅝	16	1.6	13	33.0	34	86.4
¾	19	1.9	14	35.6	35	88.9
⅞	22	2.2	15	38.1	36	91.4
1	25	2.5	16	40.6	37	94.0
1¼	32	3.2	17	43.2	38	96.5
1½	38	3.8	18	45.7	39	99.1
1¾	44	4.4	19	48.3	48	101.6
2	51	5.1	20	50.8	41	104.1
2½	64	6.4	21	53.3	42	106.7
3	76	7.6	22	55.9	43	109.2
3½	89	8.9	23	58.4	44	111.8
4	102	10.2	24	61.0	45	114.3
4½	114	11.4	25	63.5	46	116.8
5	127	12.7	26	66.0	47	119.4
6	152	15.2	27	68.6	48	121.9

ABOUT THE AUTHORS

Frank A. Droege lives in New Jersey with Anna, his wife of more than 40 years. They have three daughters: Jennifer, Jeanne, and Laura. A tool-and-die maker most of his adult life, Frank's career was interrupted when he was drafted at the start of the Korean War. He played football for the U.S. Army in Germany and later, semi-pro football in New Jersey. While working as a tool engineer, Frank developed an obsession for art and studied under Max Gothieb at Fleisher Art Memorial and at Haddonfield Art Center under George Vail.

Frank has won numerous awards for his paintings in acrylics and oils. Locally, Frank has been called a "virtual idea machine" because of his reputation for unusual mechanical creations. He designs and builds kinetic art sculptures, makes kaleidoscopes and folk toys, and also enjoys miniature painting.

Capitalizing on his various backgrounds in tools and art, Frank has entered into the professional crafts as a designer, craftsman, and author of scroll-sawn art. This is Frank's second book. His original pieces have been featured in various woodworking magazines and Frank is currently at work on two new books. His work ranges from simple mobiles to wooden reproductions of paintings by Vincent Van Gogh and Pablo Picasso. Frank's scroll-saw patterns are creations that are refreshingly original, imaginative, colorful, and are quickly becoming highly prized by woodworkers around the globe.

Patrick Spielman is the world's leading woodworking author with over 65 books published covering a variety of woodworking subjects. The new edition of his popular *Router Handbook* was awarded the best how-to book by the National Association of Home and Workshop Writers. That book and *Scroll Saw Pattern Book* have each sold well over one million copies.

A graduate of the University of Wisconsin-Stout, Patrick has taught high school and vocational woodworking for 27 years. With the assistance of his family, he has owned and operated a wood product manufacturing company for 20 years. For five years he published and distributed *Home Workshop News*, a newsletter dedicated to advancing the scroll-sawing arts. Currently, Patrick and his wife Patricia own and operate Spielman's Wood Works and Spielman's Kid Works. Both are gift galleries located in Door County, Wisconsin featuring quality products made from wood.

Over the course of Patrick's teaching and woodworking careers, he has invented hundreds of jigs, fixtures, and processes to benefit hobbyist woodworkers and the woodworking industry. He has served as a technical consultant and designer for a major tool manufacturer and he continues to pioneer new and exciting techniques for woodworkers as he has done for more than 45 years.

INDEX